Titles in the PROTEUS ROCKS series.

AC/DC
The Beatles Apart
David Bowie Profile
Kate Bush
Elvis Costello
New Wave Explosion
Hazel O'Connor – Uncovered Plus
The Police – L'Historia Bandido
Queen
Rock Bottom: The Best of the Worst in Rock
Visions of Rock
Whatever Happened to . . .?
Led Zeppelin 1968-1980

NEW WAVE explosion

PROTEUS BOOKS
is an imprint of
The Proteus Publishing Group

United States
PROTEUS PUBLISHING CO., INC.
733 Third Avenue
New York, N.Y. 10017
distributed by:
THE SCRIBNER BOOK COMPANIES, INC.
597 Fifth Avenue
New York, N.Y. 10017

United Kingdom
PROTEUS (PUBLISHING) LIMITED
Bremar House
Sale Place
London, W2 1PT

ISBN 0 906071 49 6

First published in 1981

© 1981 by Myles Palmer and Proteus Publishing Group
All rights reserved.

Printed and bound in Italy by
New Interlitho S.P.A. Milan

Picture credits:
Jill Furmanovsky 17, 21, 25, 26, 28, 32, 38, 45, 46, 49, 50, 54, 56, 58, 60, 61, 63, 70, 72, 78, 80, 82, 84, 85, 86, 87, 88, 94, 96, 97, 98, 99, 102, 103, 104, 110.
Derek Ridgers 14, 15, 42, 43, 64, 89, 90, 91, 114, 115.
Rex Features 52, 100, 101.
Thanks also to STIFF records.

Book Design by Carol Hood and Sue Peace.

NEW WAVE EXPLOSION

HOW PUNK BECAME NEW WAVE BECAME THE 80's

MYLES PALMER

PROTEUS BOOKS
LONDON & NEW YORK

	STAGNATION	9
	MALCOLM MCLAREN	17
	SNIFFIN' GLUE NEVER WRITES DOWN TO YER	19
	DON LETTS IS ABOVE CLOTHES	25
	THAT WAS THE SEX PISTOLS' WEEK THAT WAS	29
	CHAOS	33
	BUNCH OF STIFFS	35
	MARK P AND MORE PISTOLS	39
	GENERATION X AT THE VORTEX	43
	TALKING ABOUT THE PISTOLS	47
	GARY NUMAN'S MODERN WORLD	51
	THE ROUGH EDGES OF THE POLICE	53
	CHRIS THOMAS GETS THE VOCAL PERFORMANCE	55
	ELVIS AT THE DOMINION	57
	2-TONE	59
	NEW YORK NOTES i) THE SLITS AT THE RITZ ii) TALKADELIC HEADS AT RADIO CITY	63

	NEVER MIND THE PISTOLS, HERE'S THE MCCLAREN	67
	YOUR CASSETTE PET	71
	THIS COULD BE YOUR LAST COSTELLO	73
	STRAY CATS ROCK MARQUEE!	75
	IAN DURY'S FUNK ORCHESTRA ON XMAS TV	77
	TRUST SPRINGSTEEN	79
	THE ORDINARY BLOKE SYNDROME	83
	SQUEEZE GIVE THE DOG A BONE	85
	SPANDAU AND THE NEW ROMANTIC BLITZ	89
	UB40'S RUBBER BALCONY	93
	THE FINEST GROUP IN BRITAIN	95
	SEX IS HERE TO STAY	99
	ANTMANIA	105
	UK AND USA	107
	EPILOGUE	111
	INTERVIEW	116

STAGNATION

In the Sixties, when times were good, young people were looking for something heavy to get into and psychedelic rock carried messages of protest and revolution. By the mid-Seventies, times were so bad that people were looking for something light to get into.
There was a decline in music which attempted to carry any kind of message. Radical statements were out, escapism was in, and the bland were leading the bland. John Denver was big, the Stylistics were bigger, and Abba were selling more records than anyone since The Beatles. Mike Oldfield and Pink Floyd were titans of progressive muzak. The only group actually to improve over a period of five albums was Steely Dan, and theirs was a prefabricated excellence. *The Royal Scam* was the masterpiece of the ultimate Seventies studio band, but there was very little sense of a band playing, or a man singing. Many saviours were hailed of whom Bruce Springsteen was among the most interesting, but even he was a false alarm. Bruce is a good writer and a great performer, but compared to Bob Dylan he is ordinary. Successive albums by the Jamaican genius Bob Marley became alarmingly bland.
In 1975 Britain's biggest recently-emerged group was Queen, who had about as much to do with rock & roll as Charlie's Angels have to do with private detection. A quartet of university graduates, Queen were originally managed by Trident, who owned extensive sound and video studios. They were over-rehearsed, over-arranged and self-conscious in the extreme. Queen were bright, bourgeois and dull. Their albums took thousands of hours, and the lighting scripts for their stage shows were as complicated as the lighting scripts for a stage play. Freddie Mercury was about as controversial as a dead budgie.
Overall, rock music was stagnating. It had once worshipped fashion, encouraged youth, and thrived on novelty, but it had become as flabby and middle-aged as it was before The Beatles. It was as exciting as an early night, and when anything did move, it moved backwards: "WAKEMAN REJOINS YES?" and "SMALL FACES REFORM" and, even, "THE RETURN OF ACKER BILK" were among the *Melody Maker* headlines of the time.
Seventies pop had become the property of a self-perpetuating elite. When the Marine Offences Act shut down pirate radio in 1967 the BBC started Radio 1 to provide pop for the masses and music was subjected to the iron grip of the BBC Playlist. Every Tuesday at Broadcasting House five producers went into a room and decided which 40 singles the nation could hear, and if your single was not one of them, you were dead. The day-time shows were hosted by Noel Edmunds, Johnny Walker, Paul Burnett and David Hamilton, with John Peel playing a few weird cult noises after 10 o'clock at night. When former Radio Caroline jock Johnny Walker quit and went to USA in June 1976 his defection was the subject of many articles in the newspapers. Walker claimed it was wrong to use a playlist based on a chart of records people have already bought. He wanted to play a few records people might buy next week, a not unreasonable ambition. In a farewell interview with the *NME* he revealed that top disc jockey Tony Blackburn had once said to him: " 'DJ's shouldn't get involved with music.' I mean, there's a headline for you. That's one of the quotes of all time."
During the early Seventies I loved rock music, and I loved writing about my favourite groups, although I had become very predictable in my likes and dislikes. For *The Times* I reviewed The J. Geils Band, The Eagles, Bill Withers, and Procol Harum twice and The Faces twice and Van Morrison four times and Traffic four times.
Another band I liked a lot was Brinsley Schwarz. I reviewed their *Nervous On The Road* LP for Time Out, and in May, 1973 wrote a piece called 'Brinsley Schwarz: Underkill As A Way Of Life' for *Rolling Stone*. I knew the band socially and admired their struggles against the mainstream of the rock business. The Brinsleys were the obvious choice to play the private party on the night before Dingwalls opened to the public. They were sweet, funky, funny and versatile, masters of intimate performance, never too loud or metallic. They were good hippies, and they played with unfailing swing and bonhomie. They could cruise out of a country tune into a soul song and into a reggae number, and make it all sound marvellously fluent and natural. Brinsley Schwarz were the best bar band in the world.
For the *Rolling Stone* article I went to a gig at Friars in Aylesbury with them, and stayed the night at their house in suburban Northwood where the band lived along with their Irish manager Dave Robinson and assorted girlfriends. In this communal approach the Brinsleys were virtually unique in Britain. No other group liked each other enough to live together as well as work together through four albums. They were able to rehearse continuously, trying new songs out and maintaining a huge repertoire of tunes. They idolised The Band. They were a genuine ensemble in which five guys played and four sang, although Nick Lowe wrote and sang more than the others. Among other things, they were idealistic, and turned down the prestige TV show *The Old Grey Whistle Test*, because they refused to mime.
Half of the piece was taken up by an interview with the idiosyncratic and resourceful Robinson, who explained their philosophy eloquently and succinctly. The band were trying to play real music to real people in real situations rather than blitz 15,000 fans at once with a performance which would have to be loud, violent and narcissistic. Dave hated crass arena theatrics because the audience could not affect the performance in any way. Each concert by a typical big act like Ten Years After, he said, must follow a fixed formula and there was no way the crowd could take part in it or affect it unless they formed themselves into a human pyramid and started stabbing each other to death. This was a picturesque image which Dave conjured up, and for a long time afterwards I

would imagine a Alvin Lee's blues train riffing slowly to a halt as he noticed a mountain of mayhem piling up in front of him. Robinson was clearly a man who marched to the beat of his drum and he knew that some rock executives regarded him as a maverick, a likeable eccentric.

The article seemed to take months to come out, and I hated the idea of working for editors 8000 miles away in San Francisco. Also, I had not dared mention what had been by far the most interesting aspect of my jaunt with the Brinsleys. On the way back from Aylesbury that Saturday night we dropped in to visit a friend of theirs in a country house. Their friend was a crippled art teacher called Ian Dury, and we sat in his bohemian kitchen drinking tea and talking about jazz with Davey Payne, another musician. They were obviously living lives without any bourgeois comforts. I thought I knew a lot about jazz but had never heard of Earl Bostic, a legendary saxophonist they were raving about. We inspected Ian's rehearsal room which had eggboxes on the walls as primitive soundproofing.

Ian and Davey were starting their own group and the Brinsleys were helping them out with gigs and equipment. I was fascinated and arranged to see them play as soon as possible. It turned out to be a memorable occasion.

Kilburn & The Highroads played at The Tally Ho, a pub in Kentish Town, north west London, where some American boys called Eggs Over Easy had shown the Brinsleys what could be done in small rooms with tiny amps. It was the cradle of pub-rock. The Kilburns were the most ragged, delinquent bunch of freaks I have ever seen on a rock & roll stage. They were dangerously strange and subversive, vagabonds who were making raw, jagged noises. The sight and sound of Ian Dury singing a pornographic reggae song to a dozen people in a bar with sawdust on the floor was something I shall remember and treasure forever. There was only the barman and Frankie Miller, Nick, Ian Gomm, Billy Rankin, a couple of roadies and a pair of paddies and as I watched and listened I knew that this was the real underground, and that the only interesting part of the music scene was the bottom, down among the derelicts and vagrants. Where the unknown play to the uncaring, you will often hear adventurous, challenging music. On this damp wintry night it was so cold that everyone wore coats and scarves, even onstage, and the music was such a startling fusion that I knew that even if it ever found its way onto vinyl, it stood no chance of being played on daytime radio. This was truly progressive rock, but I knew that as soon as music starts to get really progressive, no-one wants to know.

Mostly, I was bored by live music. One weekend I saw Lou Reed and Captain Beefheart on consecutive nights. Reed was incompetent. The question was: can he stand up for an hour and a half after all that Scotch and mandrax? It may have worked as theatre for some, but as music it was a wretched, embarrassing, infuriating and pitiful failure. And the Beefheart gig was a fraud to anyone who had seen the phenomenal and funomenal Magic Band at The Rainbow. I hated Reed and Beefheart for inflicting such savage disappointments on me and resolved that neither would be given the opportunity to disappoint me again.

Rock & roll was caricaturing itself. Having reckoned that Humble Pie was the alltime low in raucous egotistical garbage, I then saw West, Bruce and Laing riffing desperately through *Roll Over Beethoven* and *Mississippi Queen*. They went off after 45 of the longest minutes I have ever known. I was laughing. This was the moment when heavy rock bottomed out. It was just vaudeville with volume. How did Jack Bruce get mixed up with these two turkeys? It was the most degenerate, corrupt and cynical performance I had ever witnessed, but in an odd way I was glad I had not missed it. On the way out I saw Cozy Powell and Jeff Beck and asked them what they thought of it and they both said "Bullshit!"

The rock concert as a source of stimulus and entertainment had never seemed more bankrupt. It was kaput. To use the phrase Nick Lowe used of Bad Company, it was about as exciting as a sack of rotting potatoes. Again and again I kept leaving concerts before the end. Roxy Music's attempts at ensemble playing were so dismal that I walked out on them three times. One such occasion is briefly described in one of my journals: "Dropped into The Rainbow with Stewart Joseph on the way home. It was 9.30. Roxy Music in the second of four sold-out nights were doing *Mother Of Pearl*. The set they had erected was magnificent and the lighting fancy, but the sound was feeble for bass, drs, gtr, sax and electric piano. The song ended timidly. Bryan Ferry in Valentino outfit: boots, pantaloons, white pirates shirt. A less cavalier performance it would be hard to imagine. They are not a jamming band, they can't get it on and they can't make their arrangements sparkle either.

"Shall we stay for one more song or two?" I said. "One," said Stewart.

Meet Chris Briggs in foyer, press officer for Chrysalis records, Islands chief rival among independent record companies. Not wanting to lose credibility, Chris quickly explains his presence "Richard Williams couldn't come, so there were four spare tickets. A mate at Island phoned me."

"Richard was smarter than you, then!"

"First time I saw them I said they were the worst band I'd ever seen in my life," says Briggs. "I don't know how they get away with it."

Stewart, Chris and myself were not cynics, we just liked groups who could play. The following year we drove up to Manchester to see Little Feat's first gig in England. Chris bootlegged the concert and we listened to it on the car cassette over and over again as we gunned back down the M1 at 3 a.m.

Mostly, at this time, I was overcome by feelings of déjà vu and lethargy. I had no wish to bitch in print. I did not want to chronicle my own boredom and depression in public. My general mood is evident from in this excerpt from the aforementioned journal:

"Reviewing albums is a chore. But someone's got to do it. I'd rather listen to great music than review albums because the reviewer eventually becomes the sum of his conditioned reflexes. The weekend of April 23 was a typical example. I had four new albums. *Rastaman Vibrations* by Bob Marley, and *Pressure Drop* by Robert Palmer, which was quite good a nice summer afternoon vibe. WEA had sent the Stones *Black and Blue,* and CBS had mailed me a white label of *Black Market,* the fifth Weather Report album. So I listened to the Stones twice and put it back in its sleeve.

Then I listened to Bob Marley all of Saturday afternoon until WBA came on TV and after a clumsily directed Brando film I listened to it again and again until I was yawning and there were tears of tiredness in my eyes although it was only 2.30 a.m. On Sunday I listened to Weather Report all day interrupted only by QPR 2 Leeds 0 on ITV and a couple of phone calls. I could have gone to two gigs in the evening but I couldn't be bothered. I will still be listening to *Black Market* in 1977. I am still enjoying *Natty Dread* and *Mysterious Traveller.* These records are worth more than the £3 you have to pay for them, although most records are not worth 3p. But I don't have to pay for them and luckily I don't even have to review them either.

Stick with the artist you can trust. *Desire* is a good Dylan album. *Rastaman. Black Market* and maybe three other good albums this year. There are never more than 6 good albums in any year. Take a tip from me. Listen to great music. But don't waste your time reviewing albums."

Re-reading this now, I find it lazy and decadent.

But reviewing is a search, and at the time I wanted to be in the promised land without having to go through the wilderness. I was no stoic. I had served time in the wilderness and I had worked and laboured and staggered through mountains and deserts of mediocrity. I did not want to own 5000 third-rate albums, I only needed 50 great albums and when I got sick of ten of those classics, I could replace them with ten others. Clever words are no substitute for great music. Why spoil Coltrane's *Ballads* with adjectives? Why contaminate *Highway 61* or *Astral Weeks* with mere opinions? I could listen to The Band's *Northern Lights, Southern Cross* album and know it was a classic and not care whether I was the only person in the world who was listening to it.

It seemed to me that rock had now moved so much into the public eye that it no longer belonged to the audience, but to the media. Elton John was filmed in L.A. gossiping to all-purpose TV personality, Russell Harty. What had once been the cultural expression of rebellious youth had fossilized into a chat show for Mums and Dads. Rock stars were cut off from their audience by high stages and deep oceans and were more concerned with meeting their accountants and worrying how to score cocaine on the chauffeur's day off. They had become Americanised.

Rock music had sunk to it's knees under the deadening weight of its own paraphernalia: T-shirts, stickers, passes for the artists' car park. Festivals were now one-day affairs, where you spent an afternoon behind the concrete walls of a soccer stadium and went home at 10 pm on the tube. Rock & roll was dead because all the excitement had been organized out of it. People who had been to the Isle of Wight Festivals in 1969 and 1970 were privileged. The 1970 Festival was a major event among young people. It was a youth event and a word-of-mouth event, and not just in the UK. It was talked about throughout Europe. It was not a media event, although it was briefly misreported by Fleet Street and the TV news.

Those kinds of chaotic, exciting festivals could never happen again. I had never believed that dope and rock music would save the world, but when I stood on the back of the stage as The Who's searchlights scanned a huge field of 100,000 faces and waving arms, it was strangely thrilling. I had seen a middle-aged woman and her teenage daughter rush up to Tiny Tim and present him with a bunch of flowers as he stepped from a helicopter.

These are odd flashes of memory from the distant past, vividly preserved but almost doubly remote since I never wrote them down and rarely talked about them. Some seem oddly cinematic, sharper than memories of real life: Miles Davis lying on the grass, sulking tigerishly in his shades and red sweater; Keith Moon doing a Punch and Judy show from behind the tailboard of an equipment truck, spontaneous cabaret, improvised with lunatic abandon; a crazed anarchist running onstage during Joni Mitchell's set and grabbing the mike and screaming "This is just a hippie concentration camp!" And poor Joni, young and delicately stoned, just burst into tears. Today, if the same thing happened, she would probably karate-kick him in the mouth. I recall chatting to drummer Jack DeJohnette on a sunlit backstage ramp after an electrifyingly intense 30-minute set by Miles Davis. I spent a lot of time hanging out with producer Teo Macero at the CBS recording truck.

Once, sitting round a campfire, between some artist's caravans I noticed a small compact, heavily bearded figure sitting opposite me. Jim Morrison. Later, hunched down in the same place, Jimi Hendrix. Banners and flags fluttered in the evening breeze, and in the dark distance, fires flickered on the hillsides surrounding the site. The landscape was like a massive medieval encampment, very Kurosawa.

The big moment was due late on Sunday night, after Jethro Tull. By this time the fans were exhausted. Being in a field for three days had turned them into cabbages, and ragged lines of refugee-zombies were queuing for double-decker buses to the ferry which would take them back to the mainland and civilisation.

One image, of Jimi and two film guys, was the most vivid of all. It was well after midnight and I was making my way through to a position below the stage when I looked up to see two film men, one holding a movie camera and running backwards towards me as he focused and filmed. His assistant, holding a large flash-floodlamp, was running backwards alongside him. And there,

fixed forever in a brilliant blaze of artificial light, was this impossibly exotic and glamorous superstar, holding his white Stratocaster, striding swiftly, pantherishly towards the backstage ramp. Jimi Hendrix was a giant, and he strolled on, plugged in and played the national anthem and a Beatles song simultaneously and everyone was too zonked to know how to respond. His majestic guitar filled the night. A month later he was dead.
In the six years since then I have been out to see groups four nights a week, and I've seen a lot of good ones, but I have forgotten so many faces and so many nights and so many details. It has all vanished except for a few highlights, and a few remarks. Once, after a fine day of music at Knebworth I was talking to Ian Pollock, music editor of *Time Out,* and expressed mild surprise that no English rock stars had bothered to come out to see Van Morrison and The Allman Brothers and mentioned that a couple of the Stones might have turned up and he grinned and said "They probably wouldn't dig the good vibes!"
Another time in 1972, on my first trip to USA, I was in a limousine and looked across and saw the skyscraper skyline of New York and innocently asked "Which one's the Empire State?" and Alice Cooper said "It's the one with the gorilla on it!"
Of all the many musicians I know and have known, the wittiest is Gavin Sutherland, who wrote *Sailing.* One night in Munich when I was reviewing Traffic for *The Times* the German crowd was giving Sutherland Bros & Quiver a hard time. I had been told that rock fans in Germany are into spacey things, big names and heavy metal but do not like lightweight pop-rock. This seemed to be the case. Some fans began to whistle derisively and Gavin, undaunted, said "Stop whistling at the back, it's bad manners!" and bass player Bruce Thomas said "Not only that, it's bad whistling!" After the show I strolled into the Traffic dressing room with Chris Blackwell to find Steve Winwood and Jim Capaldi angrily shouting at each other and Blackwell smoothly escorted me back into the corridor.
I saw seven dates on that last Traffic tour, although we did not know it was going to be their last tour: Munich, Glasgow, Croydon, Oxford, and the three nights at The Rainbow. At Oxford Poly they were incredible. The rapport between the musicians was sublime and they created an atmosphere of unbelievable intimacy and euphoria. I had seen Steve Winwood on countless occasions and always regarded him as the rock and soul genius of his generation but had never seen him in his sportsjacket, playing honky tonk piano in the dressing room with one of his kids frolicking in the background, and I had never heard him singing and playing off the top of his head with such casual virtuosity, such inspiration, that he created the illusion he was playing to five people in his front room, although there were 2000 fans packed into that college hall.
By the beginning of 1976 my attitude to rock music was: I've heard it, I've seen it, and it's been fun, but I am suffering from diminishing returns. I have had a good time. It's hard to imagine how anyone could have had a better time. I have been thrilled, overwhelmed and transported as well as bored, dismayed and sickened. On high nights I have seen and heard things I will never hear again, but will remember forever.
I have seen great groups on great nights. The Band at the Albert Hall. Van Morrison and the magnificent Caledonian Soul Orchestra at The Rainbow. I have seen The Faces at The Marquee with Rod running round behind the drum kit hotly pursued by a Dutch film cameraman. And even at Wembley Arena, I have seen electrifying concerts. Watching The Jackson Five from the second row was a thrill and a half. And in 1974, Jagger swanning onto the stage in his leather jacket and electric blue jumpsuit as The Stones crunched into *Brown Sugar.* Nothing in the whole of amplified music could quite equal the power and glamour of that moment. The Stones were astounding, and Mick Taylor played brilliant ribbons of splintered steel, pure guitar brilliance. I had been disappointed by Bob Marley's first night at The Lyceum but I loved him so much I gave him the benefit of the doubt and went back the second night and the music was five times better. *Stir It Up* was fantastic, a wave of warm sound that just kept rolling and rolling like the tide.
And just when I thought I had seen and heard everything, I saw a concert which was more stunning and more adrenalising than anything ever, a gig which had me buzzing for weeks. Little Feat at The Rainbow were so ballsy, but so laidback. Their music was awesomely raunchy, but subtly funky as well: great songs, ferocious guitars, dazzling keyboards and powerfully shuffling rhythms. No group with that much power ever had that much control and it was unreal to see a group which was actually better than their best records. Little Feat at The Rainbow was the rock concert of the century.
Warner Bros gave a good tour party at the American Embassy but by then I was in such a state of advanced disillusionment about the social side of being a rock critic that I could not even begin to enjoy myself. Although ultra-selective in my ligging, I still felt I had been to too many rock receptions. Larry Graham was all silver studded denim. Keith Richards face was the colour of a cheap envelope. I went through the motions. I chatted to Rod Stewart about Denis Law and a goalkeeper called Frank Haffey, and about Kenny Dalglish. Rod made a couple of cracks about Gary Glitter's "vicious" diet. I had enjoyed so many laughs with Rod and my friends and I had had so much good music and good feeling from the guy that I was depressed to find that he had now begun to bore me. I had had so much fun and entertainment from him. It was Rod who had started me off as a rock writer. My first assignment was a cover story on *Every Picture Tells A Story,* and so I had started off in Morgan Studios with *Reason To Believe* and *Maggie May* sounding wondrous on the studio monitors, and Rod, Ronnie Wood and Long John Baldry downstairs round the mike, camping around and giggling and trying to sing the backing vocals of the title track.

Rock had given me my fair share of fun, and I decided to quit while I was ahead. I have shared agonies in a Chelsea flat with the Average White Band as the luckless and unbeaten Scots soccer team were eliminated from the 1974 World Cup Finals. I've interviewed The Eagles during the recording of *Desperado*. I vaguely remember a hilariously silly night at a fancy hotel in New York with Derek Taylor, Bob Weir and his wife Frankie. I have played table tennis with Alice Cooper at his house in Connecticut. I have smoked a joint with Jerry Garcia between sets at The Lyceum, although not, let it be stressed, on the night that I was reviewing The Grateful Dead for *The Times*. I have met Mick Jagger at a party for Van Morrison. I have met Mr and Mrs Paul MaCartney at a party for Ten Years After. While other journalists queued for a phone to call in stories about how this Stones party at Blenheim Palace was not the drug orgy they had expected, I was snorting coke, gossiping with Billy Preston and having a great time.

I remember one night leaving a packed Albert Hall during a dismal Jethro Tull show and taking a cab down to the Music Workshop in Mayfair where Vinegar Joe were playing to a hundred people and asking guitarist Pete Gage what Swansea had been like the night before and he paused and thought about it and said "It doesn't get any nearer." And later I got a lift home in the van with Pete driving and Elkie Brooks and Robert Palmer in the back, banging on the table and singing swampy Dr John songs.

Thinking about this now for the first time in years, I wonder a little. I'm making myself sound like a real groupie but the truth was that I get on far better with musicians than I do with other journalists. I get on fine with stars because I can take them or leave them. Celebrities do not intimidate me at all. I met my hero Denis Law when I was 20 and made the crucial realisation that stars are just people, and since then no star has made me nervous.

My experience has been that in London they are all around all the time, so it is no big deal. I had only been in town a month in the autumn of 1967 when I went to The Speakeasy, a late-night hang-out of the rock elite. It was the age of the guitar hero. "CLAPTON IS GOD" was scrawled in big black letters on the walls of Notting Hill Gate. As I was leaning on the bar at about 1.30 a.m. I glanced over to the door and saw two slim men come in, whispering in each others ears, nuzzling each others necks like puppies. Jimi Hendrix and Jeff Beck had arrived but in that den of cool no-one even blinked but just turned away and yawned and said "Yeah, Ringo was down last night…"

One of my pet theories is that musicians are the biggest groupies of all.

When Stevie Wonder came to town to do four shows at The Rainbow I cancelled everything else and went to all the concerts and all the rehearsals and spent two nights in Basing Street Studios with him while he was mixing the tapes for a live broadcast on Radio Luxemburg. The engineer was my mate Brian Humphries, who was working for the Pink Floyd but had previously done several albums with Traffic.

Musically, those nights were among the most thrilling of my life. On the first night, with astonishing performances pouring out of the speakers, Stevie was being hyper-critical of some songs, and singing along with others, scatting spontaneously and wildly. Stevie Wonder is not only the greatest pop singer on the planet, he is so far ahead of whoever's in second place that it is hardly worth discussing.

The band he was touring with was one of the finest ever assembled, with Reggie McBride on bass and the ultra-dynamic Ollie Brown on drums, and the best three backing singers I have ever heard: Lani Groves, Shirley Brewer and Deniece Williams, later a solo star in her own right. Stevie had tapes of four whole concerts and they included some magical new songs like *Sky Blue Afernoon* and *No News Is Good News* whose melody I can still recall six years later. As far as I know neither of these songs was ever released although I read somewhere that the Jackson Five recorded *No News*.

On the second night a strange scene developed. Eric Clapton and Pete Townshend kept phoning up and asking Stevie to come over to their studio to put some electric piano (or maybe it was clavinet) on the track of *Pinball Wizard* which they were recording for the film soundtrack of *Tommy*. Stevie was busy and said he would only do it if he could be in the film. So at some very late hour (about 3.30 a.m.), the Townshend/Clapton entourage arrived bringing their 24-track master tape with them, and they sat outside drinking brandy from paper cups and not being allowed in.

So I went out and chatted to them. Clapton recalled seeing Stevie at The Talk Of The Town and being amazed by his 16-year old bassist who later left to join Miles Davis. We talked about Marlo Henderson, the guitarist who had played the first two shows but had missed the second pair, having had to fly back to USA where his wife was ill. I wondered whether Eric would have agreed to deputise for Marlo at short notice, if he had been asked. "You're joking!" said Clapton "I'd have run all the way!" In later years I often pictured Eric doing an emergency sprint down the M4 with his guitar case in hand. Who soundman Bob Pridden was there and he told me about a time when Pete was really drunk and out of his brain and admitted to Bob that he had once spent all night in a hotel corridor, just so he could meet Georgie Fame. Which confirmed what I had always believed. Musicians are the biggest groupies of all.

I remember the day The Rainbow closed for the second time. The final concert was a live recording of five or six loser groups on Island, Virgin and Chrysalis, and it was always likely to be one of the non-events of the year. Frankie Miller came on to sing with Procol Harum and they were immensely exciting for about 15 minutes before collapsing into an under-rehearsed shambles.

We were extremely bored and depressed that day. I was sitting around with Chris Briggs, NME journalist Pete Erskine and guitarist-songwriter Phil Rambow, and we were trying desperately to entertain each other. At one point towards the end of the evening I said "I really must look around for another stance on this whole rock scene. I've used up cheerful cynicism." and Phil said "You're kidding! What other stance is there? *Distraught* cynicism?"

It was time for me to move onto other things. I was a rock fan who could write and had drifted into rock journalism. I had no thought of making a career out of it. It was just something I could do, like playing table tennis. I had no thought of making a career out of playing table tennis, either. Rock music had been my guiding passion, but the cycle I had been through with it was one which many people go through with many obsessions. I had found it exciting at first, then enjoyable, and I had continued to ride it for all it was worth. Soon my nonchalance turned to disillusionment and eventually I reached the point where the only fun I got out of it was negative and sarcastic. I enjoyed *not* going to see the Pink Floyd at Knebworth, and *not* going to see Ken Russell's film of *Tommy*. While I still liked music and musicians, they had lost their ability to surprise me. There was no mystique in it any more. There was no-one I wanted to meet or see, let alone anyone I wanted to review or interview.

One of the lowest points of my disenchantment came one evening at a cinema in Leicester Square with the premiere of *The Song Remains The Same*. The film was a colossal drone, visually and musically. The music was so dull that if an unknown group had taken a tape of it to a record company they would not only not have got a deal, they would have been thrown downstairs. I was with a very bright, amusing record company secretary called Maggie, and if I had not had her to talk to I would never have got through it. "What a big wank!" she exclaimed in total disgust. I remarked that Little Feat should do a 45-minute support movie and blow Led Zeppelin off the screen every night. Never was the expression dinosaur more appropriate. It was the most dismally lethargic succession of images I have ever seen.

This, truly, was the movie of an extinct species.

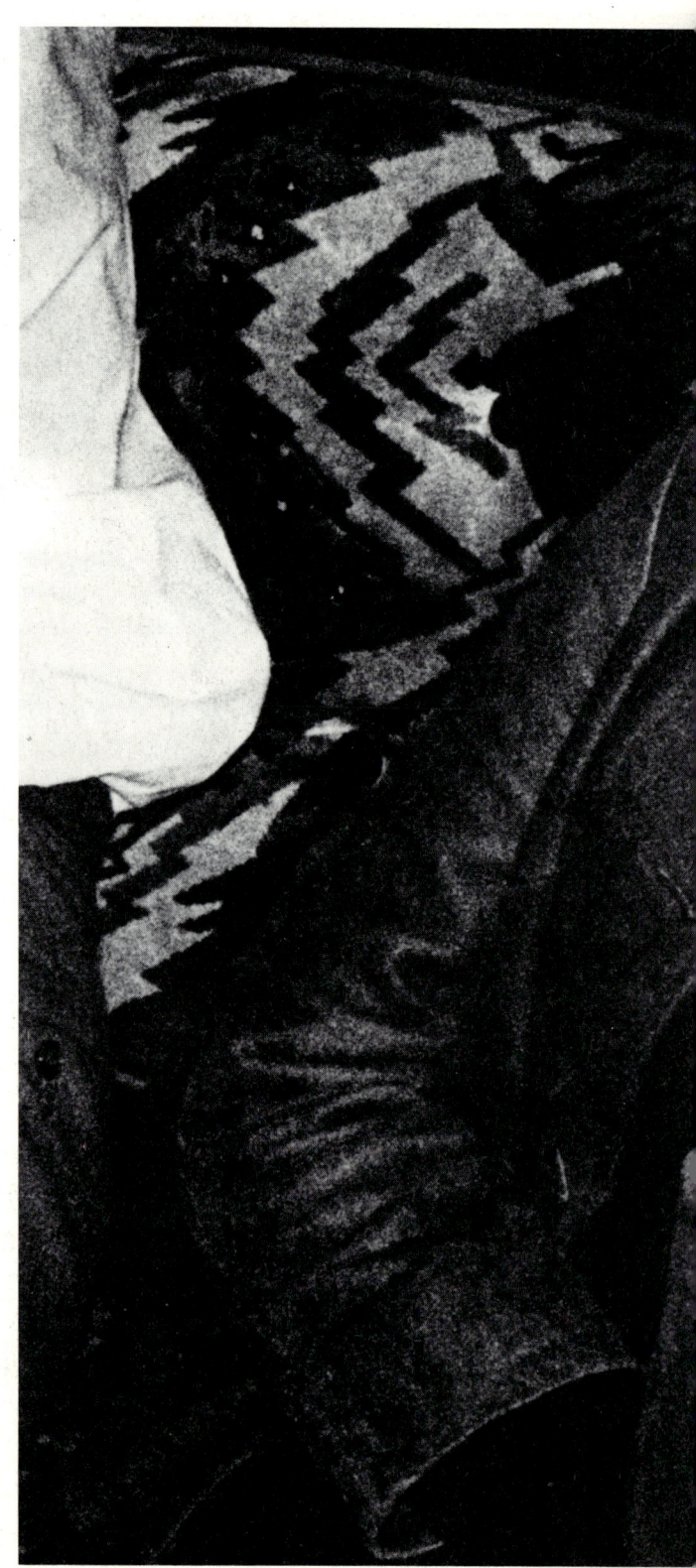

MALCOLM MCLAREN

In the beginning, there was Malcolm McLaren.
He was a Jewish kid whose academic record was unusually poor. He only got two 'O' levels and left school at 16. Not being too keen on the idea of hard work, he spent an astonishing total of eight years at various art colleges, financed by local authorities and his granny. At Croydon art college he tried to make a film about Billy Fury, his favourite English rocker.
He used his grant to buy up pram-loads of old Fifties rock record's (45s and 78s) from street markets like the one in Brick Lane, Bethnal Green, East London. Then, in the late Sixties, he opened a record shop in the Kings Road. He also sold Teddy boy clothes. The shop was called Let It Rock and many of his customers were hard-core Teddy boys, and musicians. Iggy Pop and his guitarist James Williamson were in town recording *Raw Power,* and used to come in a lot. Malcolm used to throw them out because he thought they were hippies.
Then one day in 1973 The New York Dolls traipsed into his shop in their stack-heeled boots. McLaren was amazed by their appearance and attitudes. He had always realised the crucial importance of visual style, and later socialised with the Dolls in New York but was less than struck by their music until one day he realised that sloppy playing and three-minute songs with urban lyrics had a future. By the time he became their manager, the bass player was an alcoholic and the drummer was a junkie, and new York had tired of trash and flash, preferring the more ascetic/poetic look of Patti Smith and Television's Tom Verlaine. It was now smart to be minimal. The Dolls were doomed, regarded as last year's dumb drug casualties, last year's glitter garbage, a typical American caricature. Just as Jayne Mansfield was a caricature of Marilyn Monroe, and Bette Midler was a caricature of a drag queen, so The New York Dolls were a caricature of The Rolling Stones, and not thought to be important in themselves.
In a typically bold move, Malcolm attempted to revive their flagging career by persuading them to go onstage wearing red vinyl suits in front of a big red hammer and sickle backdrop. He was keen on the Situationist politics of confrontation and controversy, and liked events and gestures which polarized attitudes. Unfortunately, America was not ready for Marxist glitter rock, and the group broke up. Malcolm told everyone that it was a tragedy and The New York Dolls were years ahead of their time.
Back in London his shop was now called Sex and specialised in bondage gear and leather. A kid who hangs out a lot at the shop is Steve Jones, who knows that Malcolm is a member of the Speakeasy Club, and wants the boutique owner to get him in. The Speakeasy is a late night disco-restaurant formerly favoured by top rock stars, but by this time it was thoroughly squalid and had been taken over by roadies, whose idea of a laugh was to blow their noses on a paper napkin and thrust it in your drink.
Steve Jones was an illegitimate working class hoodlum who was heavily into car stealing, and who had been sent to an approved school. With his mate Paul Cook he claims to have dismantled a drum kit from Hammersmith Palais and carried it out to a stolen mini-van. After that they pinched some amps and cymbals. Their larcenous acquisition of equipment reached its peak one night at the Hammersmith Odeon, where David Bowie was doing his last Ziggy Stardust shows; they sneaked in with their wire cutters and stole 13 microphones, 16 guitars and Mick Ronson's Sun amp.
Thus equipped, they begin to rehearse as a trio in a warehouse in Hammersmith with Glen Matlock on bass, playing Sixties songs, mostly by The Who and Small Faces. They ask McLaren to help them out, and Cook thinks that Malcolm only agreed to get involved because another boutique owner, Tommy Roberts, talking about finding a group to manage. Roberts, of Mr Freedom fame, is later manager of Kilburn and the Highroads for a short time.
Then they meet John Lydon in the shop and Steve gets John to audition signing along with the jukebox, and they wheel him down to the warehouse where John is shocked by the sound of his amplified voice. He had never even thought about singing in a group before. By now McLaren is encouraging them to write their own songs about their own attitudes and concerns. Musically, Matlock is the creative one, and Lydon the poet who begins to write abrasive lyrics.
Their first gigs in November 1975 are amateurish, but Malcolm sets about creating a cult around his protégés. He is acquainted with artist and socialite Andrew Logan, whose annual Alternative Miss World competition provides a freakish cabaret for the arty and decadent set; people who are fascinated by any kind of sub-Warhol scene.
In February 1976, instead of the usual drag queen contest, Logan's party in his dockside loft featured an exciting and different teenage rock group, The Sex Pistols. People were amused and intrigued by the singer's name Johnny Rotten. One of Malcolm's old art school pals, Jamie Reid, was busy creating the graphic and typographic personality of punk with collages, stencils and newspaper lettering torn out and pasted down like the ransom notes of kidnappers.
At the party, McLaren wears his beret and the boys play three shambolic sets, which consist, according to eyewitness Nick Kent of NME, mainly of the Stooges' *No Fun* played over and over again.

Sniffin' Glue
Never writes down to yer

"The Ramones were in London this month and to realy get into the fact we've put this little mag/newsletter together. Its a bit amatuer at the moment but it is the first go isnt it, I mean we can't be Nick Kents over night can we."

These were the first words of *Sniffin' Glue,* the first punk fanzine, written by Mark P. in his debut editorial, and he wasn't kidding about it being amateur. The publication was Xeroxed and its 8 pages were held together by a single staple in the top left corner, and it was all about The Ramones, Eddie and the Hot Rods, Blue Oyster Cult, and The Flamin' Groovies. On the masthead was scrawled "SNIFFIN' GLUE AND OTHER ROCK 'N' ROLL HABITS FOR PUNKS! No. 1 of many, we hope!"

This was a typical album review: "RUNAWAYS (Mercury – import) I've always hated girl bands, singers etc. Rock 'n' roll's for blokes and I hope it stays that way. Girls are good for one thing and one thing only – going shopping for glue. This album though is an exception. I realy think its got something." Mark approved of the 101ers Chiswick single Keys To Your Heart: "This is a realy good song done realy well by a great band. Rock 'n' roll/boogie-woogie at it's sweaty best. They're not a heavy band so they rely on sharp and crisp playing."

The last page was a rallying cry. "This thing called punk-rock. The weekly papers gave the Ramones a hard time didn't they 'cause they don't f'ing understand that's why. They put down their songs, stances and even their enjoyment. The reviews of the Ramones gig just sums up the whole dumb attitude of the 'best sellers' towards punk-rock. They treat it like some kind of freak show to be laughed at, I don't know why their bother. One papers gonna have 'An A-Z of Punk Rock' next week just to be hip – why dont they stick to their Queen and all that trash that drive around in expensive cars. The weeklys are so far away from the kids that they can't possibly say anything of any importance to punk-rock fans. I can't spell, I wouldn't win any awards for literature, but at least I don't write down to yer!"

Overnight, Mark P became the spokesperson of youth. He had perfect credentials. He was 19 and had quit his boring job in a bank and was unemployed and living in a council flat in Deptford, South-East London with his Mum and Dad.

"Nobody can define punk rock, it's all about rock in its lowest form – on the level of the streets." wrote Mark. "Kids jamming together in Dad's garage, poor equipment, tight clothes, empty heads (nothing to do now you've left school) and model-shops. Punk-rocks all those things. Shit, there's something happening in London now. We've had some incredible gigs and great scenes. London's got a *scene* goin', we don't need New York we've got it here. the Sex Pistols, Eddie & the Hot Rods, The Damned, Violent Luck (now called Sister Ray), the Stranglers, the Vibrators and the tasty Roogalator to name but a few. "We've got to make somethin' real happen here. Most British rock is past it now but the punk scene isn't. Let's build up our own bands instead of drooling over the NY scene. I'm not putting that scene down but if we've got somethin' goin' on here we wanna make it better. We're gonna try to do a bit for the scene but it's all up to you – the kids (and of course the guys who feel young). London punk is great so let's go."

This was pure unadulterated and unedited Mark P. in his own write and his own spel and underneath someone had scrawled "THE DAMNED ARE GREAT" in magic marker and such scribbles were the only illustrations. There were no pics or cartoons. Mark had not yet discovered that photocopying machines will reproduce contrasty black and white photos quite effectively.

The boy's offhand charm continued into his August editorial. "Funny, my piece in SG No 1 was realy easy to write. I went on about SG's place in today's society and how we're better for you than the weeklies are. Now, in this second issue I've got nothing at all to talk about." So he described the contents of SG2, and then congratulated himself. "See I've completed my column, it's F'ing easy once you get going. I hope you like the first issue and I hope you like this one more, if you dont you can go and read the MM or some other shit and die just like 'em." The enemy was being identified and hammered, and the prose style was so artless, so guileless that it was impossible to dislike or disbelieve. Punk prose did not make illiteracy respectable, but it did make it unimportant. Punk prose was a question with an exclamation mark, and Exclamation Mark P. was giving out the gospel to his disciples out there in the teenage wastelands of England. Sniffin' Glue was the tattered newssheet of underground freedom fighters.

SG 2 found Mark taking a ride down to the coastal town of Hastings with Eddie and The Hot Rods. It was fun. Roadie Dean opened beer bottles with his teeth, and obviously if the roadie had been called George and had opened the bottles with a bottle opener it would not have been half as good. Singer Barrie Masters drove the van. Young bassist Paul Gray said he was into the MC5 and The Stooges

The gig was a big success. "Every move Barrie made was cheered, when he and Dave did the leapfrog bit in *Cruisin' In The Lincoln* the mob went crazy! This is where rock 'n' roll realy counts, at the end of a pier in front of rock-starved kids." *Cruising In the Lincoln?* It all sounds very American doesn't it? Here the form/content dilemma of punk was highlighted. High-energy R&B bands had the performance panache, but not the social protest lyrics. They had the style, but not the subject matter. Some punks felt that Dr Feelgood and The Rods were allies, since the distance between amphetamine R&B and punk was less than the distance between punk and anything else. Others felt those bands were redundant relics from an era when the stones and The J. Geils band had done the same thing ten times better. The Damned were damned as cabaret punks, and took a lot of stick from earnest socio-political types who believed the punk crusade was devalued by four lunatics taking the mickey.

The next issue had a big interview with The Damned, and Marks editorial began as follows:

" 'Allo, this is the third issue and this is where we either go stale or really bowl you over. I don't like the mag…it should be fucking fantastic, but it's just cruising at the moment. There's somethin' new in this issue, we've got photos."
I was bowled over by the photos and the fact that Mark had apparently learned how to spell "really."

"Get along and see all the punk rock you can cause that's the only way somebody's going to be interested in opening some sort of club, for these bands and others like 'em. I may be sounding dramatic but I wanna go out and hear the sounds that I like every night, I wanna have to choose what gig to go to. We *need* somethin' happening daily, if it don't get that way we can forget the whole thing right now."
Damned singer Dave Vanian said he was still working as a grave-digger and mouthy drummer Rat Scabies revealed that they were "ready to play anywhere that'll have us except pubs" and said that the members of The Damned hated each other and never saw each other socially at all.

SG: What about that stunt at the Nashville, you know, kicking the drums?
Rat: It wern't a stunt, we was playing so badly well I was anyway and that number just wern't goin' right. I couldn't take anymore, it had to stop and I knew that once I got rid of that initial outburst it could go a bo bit better which it did. Except S.A.L.T. (the support group) closing the curtains on us, we was into our last number when they done it as well. Then again, it looked good, I suppose. It was a laugh afterwards, you expect hippys to be friendly people but…
SG: S.A.L.T. really wanted to get you off…
RAT: …Cause we was too much of a threat to them."
Everyone agreed that the one vital necessity was a punk club in London with groups playing every night. The shortage of places to play was chronic, and The Damned blew out their manager Andy Czezowski in favour of Ron Watts, the rolypoly booker of the 100 Club, presumably because he could get them gigs. This is typical of beginner groups who think that anyone who can get them gigs is a good manager. If they have a gig to plan for, rehearse for, dress for and talk about they are happy because they know they will be playing and working and fighting the good fight, and getting their rocks off emotionally. Before long The Damned were recording their first single *New Rose* for Stiff, produced by Nick Lowe, who was one of the few musicians around this scene who had much experience of studios.

A special issue, SG3½, celebrated the September 100 Club Punk Festival. Some festival! This event consisted of a mere two nights in the funky club in Oxford Street, which usually featured mostly jazz and blues in a long, barely furnished basement room with a late bar.
On the first night (Monday) the bill was Subway Sect/Siouxsie and The Banshees/Clash/Sex Pistols. The Subway Sect had begun as a trio busking in Hammersmith Subway with Vic Goddard singing, Rob Miller playing guitar and drummer Paul Smith banging a tin can against the wall, doing a couple of Velvet Underground numbers. There was no way a group could be more street than that.
SG's co-editor Steve Mick reported: "This was their first gig and I loved 'em. They chew gum onstage and look vacant. The 4 songs they did were great…
"After the Sect's set the buzz was going round about the Pistols follower, Sid who was gonna play drums with the next band up, Suzie and the Banshies. Everybody was excited and thought that Sid was gonna pull out his chain and madly lash out at the poor drums. When they finally made it onstage, Sid was terrific, he kept a real clear drum tempo going which really lifted the band a cut above a few other punks currantly on the scene. The amazing thing was, Sid had only been playing the drums for one day. I spoke to Sid afterwards and he was really pleased and told me he enjoyed himself.

"A few people spotted in the bar after Suzie's set were Paul Weller, the Jam's guitarist and Mike Spencer, the New Yorker who used to 'front the Count Bishops. He reckons that the London punk scene is far superior to the scene in New York. Very true."

The Clash were reckoned not to have found their audience yet but were considered to be "Probably the most powerful band on the scene at the moment."

"During the interval The Sex Pistols showed up. I approached Johnny Rotten, who was slouched over some chairs with Glen Matlock.

SG: Would you do Top Of The Pops?
Rotten: Great, why not? Should be good.
SG: There's a rumour going around that your song *Anarchy In The UK* **was made just to promote Malcolm McLaren's 'Anarchy' shirts, is that right?**
Rotten: No that's just other bands jealous of us...anyway the song came out first!
SG: Yeah, but it's said that it was all planned.
Rotten: Well, all can say to that is 'Yawn'!
SG: Just 'Yawn'?
Rotten: Yes!

"The Pistols were fucking brilliant. They were really on form, there was kids on chairs, tables...the following they've got is amazing. No one in their right mind could say they can't play, they're getting better every gig. No, there was no violence, they just played."

The second night kicked off with a silly French group, Stinky Toys, whose girl singer did versions of *Substitute, Under My Thumb* and David Bowie's *Hang On To Yourself.* Then came the noisy, crazy Damned. Bryan James broke some strings and took 15 minutes to re-string his guitar. Dave Vanian threw beer

into the crowd. Then some delinquent moron threw a glass which shattered and hit a girl in the face and an ambulance came to take her to hospital and it was later discovered that she had lost an eye.
The Vibrators were a drone, old rockers jumping on the bandwagon, nothing to do with punk at all. Next to play were The Buzzcocks, who at this time were embryonic Pistols imitators.
"Everyone seemed to have gone home for The Buzzcocks. It left us the chance to really listen to 'em. Their sound is rough, very like the Pistols but that guitar sound! Fuckin'ell it was a spitting, rasping monster. The Buzzcocks were OK they fucking done well. They are Howard Devoto – vocals, Pete Shelley – guitar, Steve Diggle – bass, and John Mayer – drums. They've got a loyal following up in Manchester and they're hoping to get some more gigs in London."
The tragic accident forced Ron Watts to ban punk from the 100 Club, but Mark refused to believe it was the end and insisted that punk was the most exciting thing to happen in British music for at least ten years. From these chaotic beginnings a few crusaders hoped to build a better tomorrow.
"I don't wanna see the Pistols, the Clash etc turned into more AC/DCs and Doctors of Madness, "wrote Mark." This new wave has got to take in everything, including posters, record-covers, stage presentation, the lot! You know, they'll be coming soon, all those big companies out to make more money on the 'new young bands.' Well they can piss off if they're hoping to tidy up the acts for the 'great British public.' The Pistols will be the first to be signed and I know that they'll stay like they are – completely independent!
The Clash, with lettering sprayed and stencilled on their clothes, appear on the cover of *Sniffin' Glue* No. 4. Their interview is the longest ever to appear in SG. As usual Joe Strummer talks a lot but has nothing to say: "I hate apathy, I hate ignorance, every group except us is rubbish, and every record anyone plays me at their flat is shit." The usual dumb rap.
Mick Jones reveals that he has had a three hour shout-up with Bryan James, "'cause he stands for enjoying himself and I stand for change and creativity." Mick continues: "Some people change and some people stay as they are, bozos, and they don't try to change themselves in any way."
Eddie & the Hot Rods? "I think they're a load of bozos and they're not telling their audience to do anything other than stay as they are. They're playing old stuff and I don't think much of their originals. The situation is where the Hot Rods audience are bozos, and it's easy to identify with a bozo."
This was fair comment, in fact. The Rods had no songwriter in the band until former Kursaal Flyer's guitarist Graham Douglas joined and wrote *Do Anything You Wanna Do*, one of the classic singles of the period. SG did not, unfortunately, ever tell us what the Rods thought of The Clash's originals.
Asked what the scene needs now, Jones says "Ten more honest bands," and Strummer says "More venues."

THE CLASH

SG told its readers not to request issues they had missed: "Don't bother writing after back issues 'cause we ain't got none! I don't believe in old news, we gotta think ahead!" Co-editor Steve Mick warned against the media's lies and exaggerations. "If you wasn't at the 100 Club Punk Fest. and you read all that shit in the press about fights, blood and bottles you would be scared shitless. Fuckin'ell what was Giovanni Dadomo (of the NME) talkin' about? It sounded more like a feeble description of The Battle of Hastings, everybody thinks of murder and massacre whenever punk-rock's mentioned now! Three beer glasses were thrown by some idiot – alright, that was bad – but that can happen and does happen at many 'hippy' rock concerts. It's just stupid, that's what it is, to blow up the violence on punk-rock and so badly to distort the truth!"

His editorial concludes: "Anyway, hope you enjoy this issue, punks have been telling us we've got the best mag around. Well, of course we have 'cause we're broke, on the dole and live at home in boring council flats, so obviously we know what's goin' on! See you soon . . ."

He may have been serious here, or he may have been sending himself up. It's hard to tell, although I am not inclined to give the earnest punks the benefit of the doubt. On the whole, they mean it, maaaaaan! Anyway the lads produced five issues from Deptford, another four c/o Rough Trade, the import/new wave record shop in Notting Hill, and then moved into Miles Copeland's (now manager of The Police) offices in Dryden Chambers in Oxford Street, a location which was a hive of punk activity.

There was an agency, a press office, a management office, and the HQ of Copeland's small record labels, all in a few small, busy rooms, and it served as a nerve-centre and rendezvous, being handy for The Vortex (just round the corner) and The 100 Club (just over the road) and Trident Studios cutting room. There was so much slanderous graffiti gossip in the loo that it took newcomers ten minutes to take a leak. Mark and his fastmouth pal, Danny Baker, were always there, as were Sham 69, Squeeze, Sting and Stewart from The Police, groupies, liggers, foreign journalists and film crews. Young kids with demo tapes sat on shabby sofas next to piles of tattered fanzines and bios, amid incessant shouting and ringing of telephones.

The do-it-yourself ethic prevailed everywhere. Mark advised in SG 5: "All you kids out there who read SG, don't be satisfied with what we write. Go out and start your own fanzines or send reviews to the established papers. let's really get on their nerves, flood the market with punk-writing!"

The issue included a rave review of Chelsea at the Electric Circus in Manchester, although the hot news from the fast-developing scene was that Gene October had left and Billy Idol had taken over lead vocals, with Tony James on bass, John Towe on drums and new boy Bob Andrews on guitar and the band were now calling themselves Generation X.

Don Letts is above clothes

Andy Czezowski was an amiable Cockney whose enterprise gave punk it's first permanent home.
The Roxy was formerly a gay club in Neal Street, Covent Garden before Andy turned it into a rendezvous for blank and spiky teenagers. In any year in any decade there are hundreds of footloose suburban kids on the streets of London's West End, looking for action, something different, exciting and preferably cheap and 1976 was no exception.
Most of the original fans came from square London suburbs like Bromley, where entertainment choices were almost nil and youth had more time to be bored, alienated and restless. At The Roxy these kids could meet others who considered themselves rebellious, and take part in an underground scene where bands and kids were re-writing the rules of rock and roll energy exchange. The audience became part of the show as never before.
Punk fashions took the form of zany hairstyles, ripped T-shirts, trousers with 17 zips, safety-pin jewellery, and dustbin-liner skirts with fishnet stockings. Black was the favourite colour, hard-wearing leather and denim the favoured fabrics. Studs, chains and badges were added emblems of identity and machismo. Even the punk girls liked to look fierce.

ENTRANCE TO THE ROXY

In this bizarre nursery Andy installed rastafarian Don Letts as disc jockey. Don had previously worked in the rag trade, and was manager of Acme Attractions, a boutique in the Kings Road, where he played music in the shop. He had no previous experience as a DJ. He had met a lot of punks at Boy, a neighbouring boutique, and sympathised with them. Despite the doubts of his black friends, he accepted the Roxy offer, and became a key figure on the scene.
All the early punk bands played The Roxy : The Sex Pistols, The Clash, Jam, Siouxsie, Buzzcocks, Generation X, Slaughter and the Dogs, Eater, The Slits, The Subway Set, among others. American acts such as Wayne County and The Heartbreakers also appeared.
In the early days there were very few appropriate records available for Don Letts to play between the groups. Fans heard a bit of Iggy Pop, The Velvet Underground, Eddie and the Hot Rods, and then it was back to Lou Reed again. None of the groups did long sets, either, since they were fast and furious players, and too new to have had written an extensive repertoire of original material.
Don was interviewed by his pal Mark P in Sniffin' Glue No. 7:
"Like, to me, the reggae thing and the punk thing…it's the same fuckin' thing. Just the black version and the white version. The kids are singing about change, they wanna do away with the establishment. Same thing the niggers are talkin' about, 'Chant down Babylon,' its the same thing. Our Babylon is your establishment, same fuckin' thing. If we beat it, then you beat it, and vice versa.
"'Cause like Johnny Rotten was telling me the other day. He's walkin' down the street now and the cops are hittin' on him. Takin' him in the van and tryin' to bust him for this and that. 'Cause of the way he looks…It's the same shit we go through. Like with me hair, and the red, gold, and green. Copper stopped me in me car and tell me I should walk!
Cause like he said, "People with red, gold and green hats shouldn't have enough money to drive flash cars" and all this crap, you know?
"And, like it's fuckin' heavy. Once you put that hat on your head you're takin' on a whole lot of shit, you know what I mean? Same as a punk, right, a punk wears his clothes. He's makin' an outward sign he's rebelling."
Don said that at the club he was getting more kids asking him for reggae than punk. "At first I wasn't sure whether to play it or not but then again, there ain't enough punk material out. Like, they say I'm DJ'ing at The Roxy…there's no DJ'ing to do. You got like 10 LPs, right, and about 20 singles and that's it. How the fuck can you DJ? You just rearrange it every night. I had to pad it out with something and I can't stand soul, the soul right now. The soul now is, sort of…money inspired. I prefer punk rock to that shit." I prefer most of the white music now to most of that shit.
Reggae had become fashionable and hip and was now being patronised by college girls, something Don found disgusting.

SID AT THE ROXY

When it all started off I was amazed, I never seen any movement move so quick, right, tremendous potential. All the kids caught on to something, they got on to an idea. They had all this energy in 'em, which we've all got...we all feel the same pressures."

One minor event in Don's life was to assume major importance as the first 100 days of The Roxy passed quickly into legend. He had liked the Jimmy Cliff film *The Harder They Come* and fancied having a bash at filming himself. A lady fashion editor called Caroline Baker had bought him an 8-millimetre cine-camera as a present, and as practice with his new toy Don began to film the punks, and went to Harlesden to film The Clash. Soon it was reported in the papers that he was making a punk movie and everyone was asking him when it was coming out, so he filmed for three months, and as it became prohibitively expensive he had to flog off all his possessions to buy film.

In August – September, 1977, a 60-minute version of the film was shown twice nightly at the ICA (an arts complex with a radical reputation), admission 50p. It was a natural for a cover story of *Time Out:* "PUNKS HOME MOVIES." Don was interviewed and explained how it had all fallen into place.

"I found that because I was the DJ and people knew me – they thought I was a crazy nigger and they couldn't figure out why I was there in the first place – I could get what the TV cameras couldn't get; the real background, the real truth. Every time they'd announce that London Weekend were coming down to film, all the guys that are really important stayed away. The rest of the kids found some more safety pins and some more make-up and jumped around in front of the camera – and it's a real distorted view of the whole thing.

"Of course with Super-8 film you only get three-minute cassettes but the punk bands seem to cram everything into about 2½ minutes which is really fortunate for me. Even when I speak to them they seem to run out of things to say in about three minutes. It seems to be a good time for them."

The spikiest home movie of the Seventies captured an embryonic rock revolution. The footage was primitive and unique. Johnny Rotten was in charismatic form, and smoked a joint in the DJ booth, Billy Idol did a Presley imitation in the dressing room, and The Slits were featured playing at Sussex University. There were shots of kids fixing smack, fans having a bash on the Jam's drum kit, and wild, uninhibited vertical dancing, soon dubbed 'pogoing.' Verité rock had become verité celluloid almost by accident.

"The way I filmed it was the same way that punk rock evolved, saying screw the rest of it and doing it your own way. I didn't even read the instructions to the camera. At first I couldn't even afford a microphone, but then I rigged up a little thing that I gave people to hold for me – but while they were jumping up and down they'd stick it in their pockets and I'd lose the sound. In the end I saved up £60 and bought a proper mike that clipped onto the camera.

When he slagged off Caroline Coon, Mark reminded him that Coon used to go down to black clubs in the Sixties, but Don was unconvinced. "You see her with her T-shirt carefully ripped between the tits. Punk, my arse. You can tell she dresses up like a punk to go to a punk do and probably puts on a red, gold and green hat to go to a reggae do."

"It's like me cuttin' my hair to go to a white pop show. There's nowhere I don't go lookin' like this...I been to church like this, weddings, court, I ain't ashamed. I just speak and when I talk, that gets me by, not how I look. As far as I'm concerned, I'm above clothes. I don't need it no more because all the kids that come into the shop, they put so much importance in clothes. They're building up a force identity.

MP : You say that but you're selling the clothes to 'em.

Don: Yeah, I sell the clothes to 'em but I don't tell 'em the attitude in which they should put it on. Buying clothes and looking far out is cool. As long as you know where its importance lies, right. As long as you know that clothes are here and you're there and someone says to you 'Well, what are you about?' As long as you can stand there and fuckin' tell the guy."

Don was convinced that just as hippies had not managed to really change anything, so the punk revolution would inevitably fail. "Punk rock is boring me 'cause they're tryin' to tell me it's somethin' new and if it was I'd be right in there with 'em. I'd be right behind 'em...I'd be fuckin' up front! But I'm 21 and I can see it already. It's gonna come along, pass, and drop, unfortunately.

"Another thing that came up in the music papers saying that if things went right, I'd have the most valuable footage around. I really didn't think of it that way until I started showing it to people. I thought, yeah, but it's not really my thing. All my life I've been selling other people's ideas, like other people's clothes, and now I'm doing it again. As far as I'm concerned, I just recorded something that happened. The people in the film should be credited, not me. I just happened to be in the right place at the right time, which seems to be the knack with documentaries – knowing what to film and not being fooled by kids who jump in front of the camera and want to wave hello to Mum."

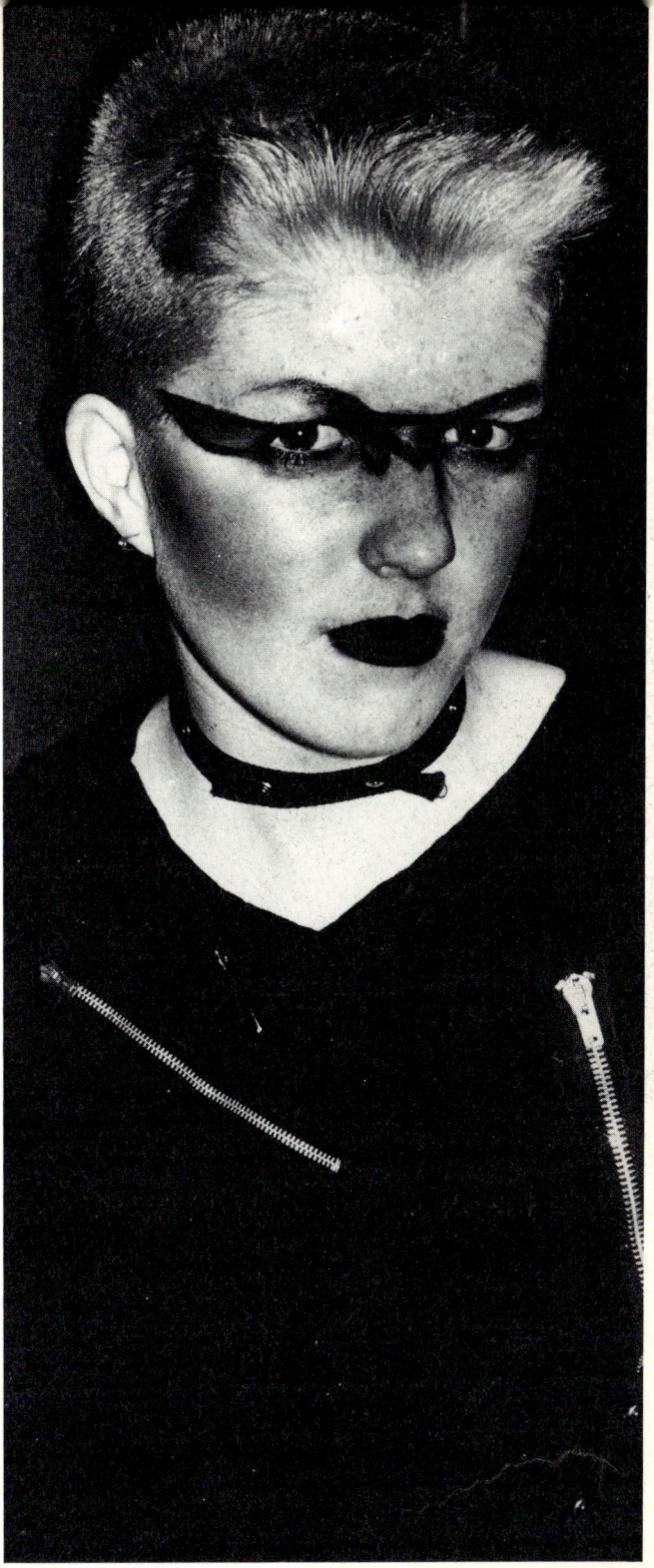

Rock and roll has never been about equipment but it had evolved to the point where Emerson Lake and Palmer had 29 tom-toms and ten synthesizers and nothing to say. It was bound to re-assert itself with minimal equipment. It did so in a small, bare concrete basement in London WC2 where young groups played music which was all content and style, and whose fuel was emotional energy, not technological hardware.

That Was The Sex Pistols Week That Was

I hate punk-rock, but I love it. It is a pose, it is bullshit, but I love it. I've done nothing but talk about it for the last seven days. All autumn I have said No Thanks, it's not for me. I hate fashion music, it will all be over by January. Punk is fun to talk about, but not to listen to. When I asked a leading A&R man if he liked The Sex Pistols he said "The group are terrible, but I like the audience." and I said "Well, why don't you sign the audience up, and do a live EP with them?"

Conflicting opinions circulate. Punk is certain to be The Next Big Thing. Punk has already peaked, it could never be more than a small cult in London. Some say Johnny Rotten is a headcase who used to go up and down the Kings Road spitting at people. Others say he is a silly little wimp, very French. He talks a good fight, but that's all.

Until last week, when punk went national; in an explosion of headlines, photos and cartoons which recalled some of the excitement of the Sixties. It was a week I shall never forget.

SUNDAY.

Watched the first in a new series of The London Weekend Show. It has The Pistols starring in a film report on punk, being interviewed by trombone-voiced, former fashion journalist Janet Street-Porter. Johnny Rotten has never been on TV before, so he doesn't quite know how to come over. He makes an effort, predictably slagging Rod Stewart and The Stones. His obscenities are bleeped out. The programme is unremarkable. My lasting impression: the earnestness of the group and their fans, their complete lack of humour.

In Britain's newspapers the establishment backlash has already begun. Derek Jewell of *The Sunday Times* writes: "Punk will fade. Its apologists are ludicrous. There are ways to protest about the putrid faces of both pop and society without lapsing into barbarism. Punk is anti-life, anti-humanity. You will probably hear much more about it, but not from me, for it will be exploited by writers desperate not to be thought 'old' and record companies without shame. When it dies, it will not be mourned."

MONDAY.

Backlash continues with *The Times* review of yesterday's programme. TV critic Michael Church is less reactionary. Admits curiosity, even fascination, but concludes "All art demands order, shape, ritual: punk rock in its present inchoate state, can only be a transient phenomenon." Late that night, I have a bath, get into bed, and start reading the centrespread interview with Rotten in *Melody Maker* which I have been meaning to read all weekend. It is the infamous I'm-not-interested-in-singing-I'm-more-interested-in-being-obnoxious interview. I read about two thirds of it. What about violence, they asked him, what about these cigarette burns on your arms and hands? What about 'em, said Johnny, "Pain doesn't hurt!" I threw the paper on the floor, put the light out and fell asleep giggling quietly into my pillow. Pain doesn't hurt! Magic! What a dynamite quote!

TUESDAY.

Get Pistols single in the post from EMI, *Anarchy In The UK*. Play it immediately, not knowing what to expect. First thought: it can't be that bad. Have a cup of tea, wake up properly, listen to it again. second thought: I'd better see them again soon, because it isn't going to last. I missed them at the 100 Club because I thought they were headlining both nights. Third thought: it's unbelievably bad, it's even worse than Eddie and the Hot Rods. Bring back The Small Faces, Slade, Alice Cooper, anything that is good noise. This is bad noise. It's not good rock shouting, it's not even a convincing sneer, it's nowhere. I remember that last week someone told me about The Damned in Aylesbury. They emptied the hall, except for a bunch of Hells Angels, who took the singer and put him in a dustbin and made him finish the set singing from a dustbin.

WEDNESDAY.

Bill Grundy (52) does a live interview with The Pistols on ITV's *Today* programme and provokes them into using a few four-letter words that everyone uses every day. Outraged viewers jam the switchboards of Thames Television. A milion people saw the programme but suddenly twenty million are talking about it. Thames broadcast an apology to viewers later on in the evening. Have resolved to buy *Melody Maker* today. See it on news stand. Front page headline: "WAKEMAN REJOINS YES." No, give it a miss this week. Do I have to choose between Rick Wakeman and Johnny Rotten? At this point, I'm sure that Rotten is the lesser of the two evils.

THURSDAY.

Fleet Street over-react hysterically. The Pistols get the front page of *The Daily Mirror, The Daily Express* and *The Daily Mail*. Mirror headline: "THE FILTH AND THE FURY!" "Uproar as viewers jam phones: A pop group shocked millions of viewers last night with the filthiest language heard on British television." The story goes on to note that "nearly 200 angry viewers telephoned the Mirror. One man was so furious that he kicked in the screen of his £380 colour TV." Page three of The Sun screams "ROCK GROUP START 4-LETTER TV STORM." I can hardly wait to dash out for the London afternoon papers. And, sure enough, they get the front page of both. The Standard: I DETEST THE SEX PISTOLS – GRUNDY. The News: WHY I DID IT – BY GRUNDY. "The object of the exercise was to prove that these louts were a foul-mouthed set of yobs."

All day, all sorts of outrageous rumours are flying about: the union have blacked the record, they are refusing to press it; the board of the parent company have put pressure on EMI Records to give the group their contract back. EMI have knights on the board, so they are super-paranoid about this sort of thing.

I wonder if the single is selling. Phone Geoff Travis a friend who owns Rough Trade, a record shop in Ladbroke Grove. He's out but his assistant tells me "We had a box, but we've only got three left. We know two other shops which have sold over 50 already. It's the fastest-selling single since Godknowswhen." I dash home. Can't wait to see The Pistols on TV's News At Ten. Sure enough, extra sensation: Bill Grundy has been suspended for two weeks for sloppy journalism. How precious can these TV companies be? What they should do is re-show the interview tonight with the swear words bleeped out, and re-book the Pistols for Friday's Today show and have ten million people watching.

FRIDAY.
Lunchtime. A friend phones: "Have you seen the papers. They've got the front page of The Daily Express again! Where can they go from here? Get killed onstage? Become a legend?" Apparently there were 35 photographers outside EMI waiting for the group to come out after a meeting. Rotten now has two bodyguards. Another friend phones: "They've got front page and centrespread of The Mirror. They've got a competition for the best punk joke. First prize, a Sex Pistols single. Second prize, two Sex Pistols singles!" That's the oldest gag in the world, I protest. "I know, but you've got to hand it to them for trying!"

Late afternoon in the advertising agency where I am working. Read art director's Guardian. Only two articles on The Pistols: "Rotten is 20, has pallied insolent looks that could replace Jagger's lips as a symbol of youthful arrogance and smears Nivea cream on his short hair to make it stick up. He and The Pistols are preparing a song called There's No Future, to the tune of the national anthem."

SATURDAY.
By now music business opinion seems to have polarized. Some people think McLaren is doing well for an art student with a few bright ideas. He can't lose, because any minute now each of the major record companies will sign a punk band and start spending money on it. So punk will become big, which will be great for The Pistols who have a head start on all the other groups.

The opposite opinion is this: if McLaren really thinks punk will be big, he isn't showing a great deal of entrepreneurial imagination. A more ambitious businessman could easily have taken the advance from EMI (said to be £40,000 but actually £17,500) set up his own label, called it Punk Records, cut singles with ten other punk bands and monopolised the excitement and profits for a while – and done albums with any of the bands which had hits.

SUNDAY.
The Sunday Times says seven dates on the 'Anarchy' tour have been cancelled, but the rest of the tour should be a guaranteed sell-out. I'm still enjoying it and I'm still intrigued by the contradictions: if Rotten does make it big and really doesn't buy a Rolls Royce and a mansion in the South of France, then surely someone, somewhere is in trouble.

And of course the social context of punk rock is very interesting. If there is a spark of authentic rebellion in the mass of Britain's allegedly alienated and unemployed youth, if the 15-22 age group really are angry and desperate for something

JOHNNY INTERVIEWED BY TV PRESENTER JANET STREET PORTER

new to relate to and imitate, if music that merely sounds good is replaced by music that has something to say, then punk could be a craze of truly phenomenal proportions. The first one for years to come from the street rather than from the business.

All I want to know for the time being is: will *Anarchy* be in the charts next Tuesday? If not, will it be the following Tuesday? Sunday December 5th 1976.

chaos

In some ways punk was not so much an explosion of music as an explosion of messages and personalities.

Among the messages were: anyone can do it, anything goes, and British is best. Suddenly anyone could perform, anyone could be a bit famous, and anyone could make records. There was a badge at the time which summed it up. It said, "I WAS WASHED UP ON THE NEW WAVE."

Record companies are always looking for new talent, and most of the responsibility lies with the A&R department, the heart of the record company. They are concerned with artists and Repertoire. The staff of the A&R department listen to demo tapes, meet groups, managers, producers and publishers, and scour the pubs and clubs in search of up-and-coming talent. They also have to work with acts they have already signed. The secret of successful A&R is not just signing the right groups, but doing the right things with the right groups. The average A&R man can easily become bogged down in his habits; the late nights and the seemingly endless incoming flow of tapes can make it a numbing occupation. Fortunately, he is invariably protected by an exceptionally charming and helpful secretary who informs callers that their demo tape was only one of 50 which arrived last week.

The advent of punk created chaos.

For a while, the record companies were bewildered. Suddenly the scene was in such a state of flux that the A&R men wondered whether it was time to dismantle entirely their whole apparatus of assessment. After years of asking such vital questions as "Can the singer sing?" and "Can the drummer keep time?" and "Can the guitarist play in tune?" they were suddenly confronted by this mass of hideously amateurish noise from dozens of young groups playing to young audiences who were loving it.

Previously, they were looking for a group which could play well, or sing well, or write well, or steal well, and if they could find a group which could do two of those four things, they would probably snap them up. Whatever the young kids felt about mad, manic thrashing noise, there was obviously still a lot to be said for good tunes, good lyrics and good rhythms.

Most of the talent was embryonic, and although the cheaply-produced singles with picture sleeves would sell 10,000 or more, there was no way of telling how these kids would develop. Most punk bands had identical instrumentation, so it was hard to tell a good one from a bad one. More than ever, the executives were watching the audience.

It soon became clear that the beauty of the punk scene was that these new groups were not obliged to compete with The Who and The Stones in American basketball stadia. So the record companies became nervous. Although signing a band can cost them thousands of pounds, not signing one can cost them millions.

When opportunity knocked in 1976-77, there were many opportunists who were not backward in coming forward. For five minutes the novelty of Tom Robinson singing *Glad To Be Gay* was fun, but he soon sank without trace. Meanwhile, Bob Geldof rose without trace. The Boomtown Rats were an Irish showband who saw their chance. The Stranglers appealed to fans who wanted to be up to date, but did not want to change. There were, however, a few eccentric talents abroad, and one of the most interesting was John Cooper Clarke, who made it as a "punk poet" although he was more of a speedfreak rock talker. This skinny spieler celebrated the life and times of an observant, sardonic loser on the streets of Manchester and district. He was new journalism and old music-hall, he was also every comedian who couldn't sing and every sensitive sixth-form Dylan fan. He was built like a matchstick and he had a lacquered barnet. One could imagine him spraying the putrid goo on his hair from a pushbutton canister and revelling in the tackiness of it.

Producer Martin "Zero" Hannett, the creative catalyst behind much of the Northern talent, recorded Clarke first for Rabid Records and then produced a CBS album called *Disguise In Love* which furnished each of Clarke's salty poems with an appropriate musical backing.

The music was astral for *I Married A Monster From Outer Space*, electronic for *Health Fanatic* and funky on a couple of other tracks, leaving Clarke acapella for *Salome Malone*. At times we can hear him sniffing and coughing. He was not cleaned up for mass consumption, but it seemed at times that John is just providing the word-track for Hannett's sound-movies. Although the production is uncompromising, there are no four-letter words. Swearing prevents radio play, but can be used in live performance, where it still has a certain shock value. When I saw John Cooper Clarke at a CND college gig he made me laugh a lot and got me high but it was all in the material rather than in the performance. Johnny Clarke is a very limited actor who can't do half as much with his face and body as, say, Loudon Wainwright, the folky American. The Clarke-Hannett partnership was almost as mutually beneficial as the Ian Dury-Chas Jankel liaison, although the bard of Salford is not a talk-singer like Dury but a speedfreak rock talker whose verbals sometimes come close to song.

The convulsions of 1976 affected musicians of all age groups. Stewart Copeland was the drummer in Curved Air who were doing nothing much and when he went down to The Roxy and encountered all this new energy, he was excited and wondered how he could be part of it. So he formed The Police with Sting, who had just come down from Newcastle and was on the dole, and guitarist Henri Padavoni and played at The Roxy, doing a load of terrible two-chord songs he had written.

The fans and press hated The Police because they were too old. They were 26-year old musicians with dyed blond hair and boiler suits, nothing to do with punk, and as such were generally despised.

Bunch of Stiffs

Around London there are always dozens of musicians who have had a taste of fame and recording but have been unlucky or silly or mismanaged.

In the aftermath of pub-rock, there were hundreds of them but most were too broke, too stoned, too drunk and too disorganized to do anything.

Stiff Records was started by Dave Robinson and Jake Riviera to make records with acts which no-one else wanted. Although chronically under-financed, they made it a success by the panache of their promotion and packaging. They were underdogs who barked louder. Their motto was If it ain't Stiff, it ain't worth a fuck."

In a daring move they took a bunch of hippy pub-rockers and gave them a haircut and launched them boldly on a tour called A Bunch Of Stiffs. The groups were a miscellaneous bunch of losers, mavericks and misfits, the dregs and rejects of the failed pub-rock crusade which had fizzled out after Jake and others had put a huge amount of righteous energy into The Naughty Rhythms Tour. This was a package of Dr Feelgood, Kokomo and Chilli Willi, three groups who could not headline on their own, and which were with three different record companies. At the time Jake was the manager of Chilli Willi, who broke up after the tour.

Robinson and Riviera had learned a lot from the pub-rock era, although their protégés had never really developed or delivered in the studio. Dave had managed Brinsley Schwarz for several years before Dai Davies took over, and Jake was Nick Lowe's best pal and flatmate. Pub-rock had failed because it had no social content, no relevance. Bands were bogged down in American influences. They either played *Six Days On The Road* or *Johnny B. Goode* and when pub-rock became pub-soul with Moon and Kokomo, they played *Ain't No Sunshine* and Aretha's *Angel*. In other words, they were competing with Michael Jackson, so they were doomed before they even started.

The Kilburns had been the most British, and the most interesting, but also the most unlucky. They did a good album on the Raft label which was never released because WEA in Los Angeles decided to fold the label, and after that they did a cheap and pathetically misproduced album called *Handsome* for Pye's Dawn label. In February 1976 they played Dingwalls as Kilburn and the Highroads but by June, significantly, they were billed as Ian Dury and the Kilburns.

The only hit record to come out of pub-rock was *How Long*, the Ace single, which gave them enough credibility to be allowed to make three albums on Anchor while all the other bands broke up after one or two. Groups, after all, had been playing in pubs in London for twenty years. Having spent millions of pounds on a series of groups which had been disappointing, the record companies blamed the press for lumbering them with a load of long-haired losers.

Anyway, everyone had learned what not to do. Stiff now took a skinny, ugly bespectacled little guy who had been turned down by every record company in England and cut an album in three days and stole Buddy Holly's image and Elvis Presley's name and did a marketing campaign which made him look even skinnier and uglier than he really was. The creation of Elvis Costello was a gamble. If it came off they would be well on the way to carving out a corner of the record business for themselves, and owning and running a record company is much more fun than managing a group since when you manage a group you are working for them, but if you hire a group to make records and give them a share of the profits, they are working for you.

A small fanatical team based in a tiny office in Notting Hill, West London, released the album *My Aim Is True*, all mail and memos and press releases being stamped with the message "DO SOMETHING FOR ELVIS TODAY." It was a job, but it was also a crusade. Jake's publicist Glen Colson talked up a storm, and I recall being shocked and disbelieving when he told me Costello was the most exciting thing to happen in Britain since Jimi Hendrix.

London in August 1977 offered consumers in clubland a wide choice of bands. You could see Squeeze at The Nashville for 75p, or Tom Robinson at The Hope and Anchor for 75p, or XTC at the Hope for 50p. For a big name thrill, you could check out Eddie and the Hot Rods who were appearing two nights at the Marquee and charging £1.25.

Elvis Costello's Sunday night at the Nashville cost those not on the guest list £1. The pub is packed and Elvis and the Attractions bounce onto the stage at 9.40 p.m. and play 45 minutes of loud, fast, monotonous music. The sound is dominated by keyboards, a Farfisa organ which sounds cheap, kitschy and different, plus a clavinet which gives them a dimension of melodrama. They are very melodramatic.

They are slick. They waste no time between numbers. After the set and the first encore they sprint offstage faster than any group I have seen since the Small Faces at Manchester University in 1966. Costello is the ugliest man I have ever seen on a rock stage. In a medium-sized pub like this everyone is close to the stage and I can see that his face is bright red and he is sweating profusely under the lights and I reckon that if Muhammed Ali was here he would say that Elvis is so ugly the sweat runs down the back of his head.

In fact, he is so horrible, I have to keep looking away, so I look at the girls in the audience who do not notice me looking at them because they are transfixed. Their eyes are glued to this spastic figure centrestage, and strangely enough, most of them are smiling.

The Attractions don't play on *My Aim Is True,* a short, rough album which was produced for £600 by Nick Lowe and on which Elvis was backed by Clover, a fact which remained a secret for a long time. Later, they held auditions and hired Bruce Thomas, formerly of Sutherland Bros and Quiver, and former Chilli Willi drummer Pete Thomas, no relation, and Steve Naive on Keyboards.

The weekly papers, particularly the *New Musical Express* are keen on anything a bit mad or over-the-top, and Jake is good copy. "I'm interested in signing lunatics" he says. "History proves that the best art comes from crazy people."

Graham Parker's rhythm section played on Elvis's *Watching The Detectives*, a magnificent song which was not given the

WRECKLESS ERIC

production it deserved. Nick Lowe's mix was raw, boomy and punky.

Before re-emerging for the Bunch Of Stiffs tour with Costello and Wreckless Eric, Ian Dury had decided to disappear and try to make a good album which he did with the classic *New Boots And Panties*, after releasing a great single *Sex And Drugs and Rock & Roll* which becomes almost an anthem for the Stiff crusade. The album is launched by Dury's personality, but sustained by Jankel's musicality. It is here that his skills as a tunesmith and arranger first come fully into focus. From the opening classic *Wake Up And Make Love With Me* (Jankel's own favourite among their many collaborations) to the gentle synth burbles of *Clever Trevor* to the jolly nonchalance of *Billericay Dickie*, the whole venture is marvellous, and it goes on selling and selling. *New Boots* becomes the most popular and definitive British album of the mid-seventies. And it is this studio success which creates the demand for a band which is named after one of the songs on the album; "Blockheads."

Ian Dury's lyrics are built to last by a craftsman who writes, rewrites, polishes, and edits until he achieves maximum memorability. If prose is words in the right order and poetry is the right words in the right order, then most rock lyrics are prose, but Ian Dury is poetry.

New Boots And Panties works because it strikes such a good balance between the singer and the band. The music is a lively and subtle embellishment for the poetry. Dury's songstories are sympathetically showcased – the album is a triumph of packaging, as well as a triumph of personality. The crippled kid from Upminster, Essex, becomes a professional Cockney in the same way that Billy Connolly is a professional Scotsman and Max Boyce is a professional Welshman.

The crossover potential of funk with Cockney lyrics proves to be huge. Dury appeals to punks and hippies, kids and parents, middle class and working class. He is a 35-year old colloquial croaker, who sings of lawless brats from council flats and his old man, the chauffeur, who does the crossword in the Standard at the airport in the rain.

When Ian Dury is the guest host of *Star Special*, a Sunday radio show on which celebrities choose their favourite discs, he plays a remarkable selection of funky and soulful records. He dedicates *One Step At A Time* by Louisiana ace Clifton Chenier to his old mate and manager Charlie Gillett, and he follows it with Lloyd and Shirley's *Queen Of The World*, a perfect illustration of how black New Orleans music influenced black Caribbean music.

Being a Beatnik, he plays some Lenny Bruce, and some brilliant jazz tracks: *Embraceable You* by Charlie Parker, some Archie Shepp and a monster Mingus track with Eric Dolphy, Booker Erving and Jackie Byard from 1953. Country is represented by Jean Shepherd's *Satisfied Mind* and Hank Williams's definitive nasal ballad *You Win Again*.

Dury says that although there is some dispute as to who was the favourite punk band, as far as he is concerned it was The Fugs and he plays *I Couldn't Get High* which rattles along with all the untidy dope-fuelled surge and clatter of those American garage bands. Great stuff. An amazing single which I had never heard before, but which I have now heard many times, since I taped the show. The next record is by music hall maestro Max Miller. Ian Dury is the only person on the planet who would play The Fugs followed by Max Miller.

"If you did nothing else but listen to good records for the rest of your life, you'd never catch up," he says. His spiel is succinct and self-mocking. In two hours he does not play one bad record. He plays a bit of Jelly Roll Morton, and some Dr. John, and one of the greatest Aretha singles, *Spanish Harlem."*

Ian Dury is the best disc-jockey in the world.

37

MARK AND MORE Pistols

In 1976 there was a war of opinion. It was a small skirmish at first, but it spread, and became more serious. The Sex Pistols were making new music for a new audience, misunderstood by the older audience, and by conservative elements in the media. One of the most comical clashes of the time was the Mark P./John Collis altercation. Collis is the music editor of *Time Out*, the weekly guide to what's on in London. Collis has a moustache and wears denim shirts and likes Buddy Holly and Chuck Berry.

In *Sniffin' Glue* No. 6 in January 1977 Mark scrawls on the front cover: "THIS ISSUE IS FOR JOHN COLLIS R.I.P." He reports how *Time Out* had asked him to write 2000 words about The Sex Pistols and he wrote just over 1000 so they wouldn't cut it down. But Collis still butchered his piece and Mark was furious and reprinted the article in full in SG:

"The Sex Pistols are gonna break all the rules. They'll bring about a change which will make the outlook for British rock music very exciting. Rock's been a 'light entertainment' for too long, it's all too safe and it's not scaring parents. They'll scare all the pathetic rock fans who've been satisfied with shit for so long. The Pistols are the most important rock group in Britain at the moment."

Mark declared that *Anarchy in the U.K.* was the most relevant rock single since *My Generation* and that: "Most kids have never experienced a feeling of unity between an audience and performer." He said that The Who were once an important group but *My Generation* is meaningless when sung by a 30-year old.

"The audience for The Pistols is waiting – out there in the discos, on the football terraces and living in boring council estates. The Sex Pistols are not a 'new fashion craze,' they're reality. If people are scared of 'em, it's their own fault, it's because they don't understand life. Life's about concrete, the sinking pound, apathetic boring people and some of the highest unemployment figures ever.

"The Pistols are helping kids to think. That's why everybody's scared, because there's some kids that are actually thinking. The Pistols reflect life as it is in the council flats, not some fantasy world that most rock artists create. Yes, they will destroy but it won't be mindless destruction. What they destroy will be replaced by a more honest creation. The likes of Led Zeppelin, Queen and Pink Floyd need to be chucked in the classical music section. Those and bands like them are composers, musicians and artistes. They've got to make way for the real people and the Sex Pistols are the first of them!"

Like all good propaganda, this was marvellously simplistic stuff. By this time EMI have signed the Pistols and they play Notre Dame Hall in London on November 15th, 1976. "The Pistols were great. After a month of recording and rehearsing they were solid as rock. A short set was done for the cameras and they came back to play a 'real' set for the fans. Rotten was fantastic, he was breaking all the rules. What other guy would just stand stage-centre after the set and clap for an encore with the crowd. He was saying how *he* wanted rock to be. No rock & roll clichés for him. He's the most honest performer around at the moment." Mark's blind adulation is almost limitless: "Steve, Paul and Glen are all honest guys, not one bullshitter among them, and this is why they'll make it."

The release of *Anarchy* is seen as a triumph. "The Pistols have won the first battle. From now they'll move on and smash every rock & roll law there is." Mark P. concluded: "I hope that John Collis is forced into retirement. May he rest in peace."

In general punk-rock was an important reversal of trends. It was a reaction against the media and the music business establishment, a revolt against the increasing Americanisation of British groups, and a return to rock & roll attempting to be socially relevant. For the first time in a long time, the groups belonged to the audience again.

The Pistols had a lot of bravado, and they enjoyed a lark, and a confrontation. They learned a lot from the furore which surrounded the Thames TV interview with cheeky Bill Grundy, who provoked them, and was then suspended when his bosses viewed a recording of the show. Malcolm McLaren realised that there are still people around who believe that a four-letter word can harm society, and that a few lads with a drum kit and two guitars can blow up Buckingham Palace.

Fleet Street had helped The Pistols to spearhead a new phase of pop history. Record companies began belatedly, to react to it. Polydor sign The Jam. CBS hold off for six months, then sign The Clash, one of whose songs is *I'm So Bored With the USA*. An explosion of young groups playing to young kids in their own backyards rescues British rock music from the suffocating and embalming influence of American showbiz.

Too often in the recent past the record companies have taken over groups too soon, and too completely. The more a company believes in a group, the sooner they begin to direct their efforts towards the USA. Record sales in UK are only 6% of the world market, and are declining, so the companies look abroad for their profits.

And, of course, America encourages giantism. The realities of mass record marketing are such that the system favours groups which can tour effectively. In other words, anyone who can get it together to look good and sound good in front of 20,000 people a night can sell a lot of albums. The concert set-up, and the radio stations, place a premium on presentation, not content.

At home the message is one of anger, frustration and alienation. The rock weeklies, *NME, Melody Maker* and *Sounds,* are quick to give more and more space to groups which carry the message. The MM cover of June 4th 1977 has the headline "STREETLIFE" and a large news picture of Johnny Rotten and Sid Vicious having a tête-à-tête with a police constable in Portobello Road. With his spiky blond hair, leather trousers and can of lager, Rotten looks as loutish as the Stones did in 1964 and as media-shrewd as Alice Cooper in 1972.

The young have always mocked their elders, but never in the

history of amplified music have they mocked them with such spleen. The lengthy interview by Allan Jones inside is somewhat less nihilistic, however, than the "Pain Doesn't Hurt" classic the previous November. But Rotten had developed into a veritable Führer of opinion. Verbally, he puts the boot in hard, and often.

Rotten begins by complaining that he is unable to get a drink anywhere in Highgate because he has been banned from all the pubs there. Then he slanders such established rock stars as Mick Jagger, Robert Plant, Ian Anderson and Roger Daltrey, with Sid occasionally joining in with a chorus of "He needs a good kicking!"

Sid is equally scathing about all their punk colleagues. "That Damned album sounds like a Searchers album. All tinny. And that Clash album sounds like a folk album." Did the Stones ever slag their rivals? Never. The Stones had their first hit with a Lennon-McCartney song.

"Of course there is no fun in being on the dole." said Rotten. "But music should offer a relief from all that. It shouldn't be depressing. If a song is about boredom, it should be about ways to overcome that boredom. It has to be true, but there should be humour. Optimism. And that's not political." As for the Chelsea single, *Right To Work* he says "That's Gene October. Him screaming about wanting the right to work is hysterical. He's got a job. He's in a fucking group. Ridiculous."

After a few more entertaining, incisive and derisive comments, Rotten observes that "We're the only honest band that's hit this planet in about a thousand million years." This remark rates as something of a landmark in self-adulating hyperbole, and one of the best since Dylan said to Keith Richard: "I could have written *Satisfaction,* but you guys could never have written *Mr Tambourine Man.*"

Already two record companies have paid Rotten to go away and stay away. In March, after being dropped by EMI, a big British label, they sign to A&M, owned by Los Angeles moguls Herb Alpert and Jerry Moss. The group are photographed at a contract signing ceremony outside Buckingham Palace. British managing director Derek Green says "I believe The Sex Pistols will effect some major changes in rock music and we at A&M are excited by them, their music, and to have entered into a worldwide recording agreement."

The *Evening Standard* soon reported "SACKED AGAIN – BUT PISTOLS GET £75,000. The group had been dropped after only seven days. McLaren said he was shellshocked after receiving a telex from LA: "The Sex Pistols are like some contagious disease – untouchable. I keep walking in and out of offices being given cheques. When I'm older and people ask me what I used to do for a living I shall have to say 'I went in and out of doors getting paid for it.' It's crazy."

After this second sensational sacking McLaren was given back the master tapes of what was to have been their first single on A&M. The song was originally called *No Future,* but he shrewdly judged that a change of title to *God Save The Queen* would have greater outrage potential. Sure enough, when it was released on Virgin, their third label in six months, the *Mirror* headline was "BAN THIS PUNK DISC SAY MPs."

In London, Capital Radio played the record until the IBA ban just before the Queen's Jubilee weekend. Charles McLelland, Controller of Radios 1 and 2, commented: "Despite the arrival of The Sex Pistols record in the charts we have no intention of playing it, as it is in gross bad taste." The single was also banned by Radio Luxemburg and by the weekly TV pop programme *Top Of The Pops.* Indeed, so infrequently was the song heard that when Radio London DJ Charlie Gillett played it on his *Honky Tonk* show one Sunday, he became the subject of a news story in Monday's *Sun.*

The media ban was one thing. The single also suffered a distribution ban. The retail chain stores of Boots, Woolworths and W.H. Smiths refused to stock the record. This saved a lot of the small shops which struggle to compete with the record counters of chain stores. The single sold 210,000 in the space of a few weeks and strengthened alternative retail outlets.

The young fans did not care that they could not buy a record they liked in the same place as their older brothers bought their Pink Floyd album, or their Mum bought her Jack Jones LP. In fact, they probably preferred it. Often the shop is a rendezvous where kids can talk about groups they have seen or plan to see, and buy badges and *Sniffin' Glue* and other cheaply-produced punk propaganda.

Clearly, notoriety can only help a record up to a certain point. When it becomes a hit, the only way it can become a bigger hit is for more people to hear it on the radio. *God Save The Queen* went to No. 2 on the main chart, the commercial radio chart in Birmingham, and on the NME chart, taken from shops other than Boots, Smiths and Woolworths, it was No. 1 for the week of June 15th 1977.

Notoriety tends to be self-perpetuating and, before long, wherever the Pistols went there was trouble. When the single was a hit they had a small party to celebrate its success on a boat on The Thames. Virgin hired the launch *Queen Elizabeth.* As the boat passed the Houses of Parliament, the Pistols began to play through a small 400 watt P.A. They had not performed in public for five months. They played *Anarchy, Good Save The Queen, No Feelings* and *Pretty Vacant.* There was a trivial altercation when a French photographer accidently elbowed Johnny Rotten in the face. A more minor fracas would be hard to imagine.

In a typical instance of hysterical over-reaction, the captain radioed for the law. The boat was surrounded by police launches, several policemen boarding the boat. Ironically, in the middle of *No Fun,* they cut off the electricity. There were brawls during the disembarkation at Charing Cross Pier, and eleven people were arrested and taken to Bow Street Police Station.

McLaren was charged with insulting behaviour intended to provoke a breach of the peace. They were jailed overnight, and appeared before the magistrates in the morning. All pleaded 'Not Guilty,' denying various charges of obstructing police, assault on police, unlawful obstruction and threatening behaviour, and were remanded on bail of £100.

A week later Johnny Rotten was recognised in a pub in Islington, North London. A group of men in their thirties attacked him, producer Chris Thomas and studio manager/engineer, Bill Price, in the car park. All three were treated in hospital. Rotten had found out that pain did hurt, after all. The papers said it was the work of monarchist vigilantes.

At this point, The Sex Pistols were at an early stage of their career. The most interesting challenges were still to come: first album, first headline tour, America. Already the New Wave is being rapidly absorbed into the mainstream of the rock business. Its long-term effect was to be a healthy one. The clandestine atmosphere surrounding The Pistols would eventually disappear. The Clash will admit they are on CBS to sell records, make money and become stars. Russell Harty will have McLaren on his chat show.

And even if many of the messages of the movement were falling on deaf ears, acceptance of punk styles was on the increase. After hippy chic, punk chic was inevitable. Zandra Rhodes' fashion safety pins were soon on sale.

GENERATION X AT THE VORTEX

It is a Monday night, about midnight, when we get to The Vortex, the club where it is all happening at the moment, the moment being August 1977. There is some mild aggro outside on the pavement. The security gorillas dwarf the tattered kids and as we arrive one of them is shouting "WHEN I SAY THERE'S NO RE-ADMISSION I MEAN THERE'S NO FUCKING RE-ADMISSION. YOU CAN GO OUT BUT YOU CAN'T COME BACK IN, ALRIGHT?"

"That's me," I say, helpfully, pointing to my name on the typed guestlist in his hand.

"You can read, then?" says the gorilla.

"Chris Briggs," says my companion.

"Sorry, someone's already been in on that name."

Chris produces a white card which says Chris Briggs, Chrysalis Records, and says "I'm the guy who is writing the cheque for that guestlist tomorrow."

The bouncer shrugs, grins, and motions us downstairs into a dark labyrinthine cellar, crammed with 800 punks. There are spiky heads, safety pins, chains, studs, black leather and shredded, stencilled T-shirts everywhere. With this scene, and four groups for £1, The Vortex appeals to the younger fans who don't mind discomfort: there is so much steam coming off the walls, it's like walking into a kettle.

The record playing as we walk in is *Anarchy In The UK*, withdrawn by EMI and now being imported from France where it was released on the Barclay label, and sold for £1, compared to 70p for a regular British single. We have just come from watching Little Feat at the Rainbow, the first of four nights, so we have missed the first two bands. After a few reggae records, Adam and the Ants come on. They are a typical wall-of-noise fourpiece with a useful Freddie Mercury type vocalist camping around adequately.

Unfortunately, the band is terrible, especially the drummer. After the giant sound of Little Feat, it's like a sparrowfart.

As Briggs goes into the toilet, he meets six punks scurrying out. Two ridiculously drunk and hostile Scotsmen are in there saying "Anybody comes in here hasta take us on!" and Briggs says "Gimme a break lads!" and has a piss and walks out again past the pair who are still holding each other up and shouting "Anybody comes in here hasta take us on!"

Tonight is an important moment in Generation X's career, their first London date after signing a record deal. Lead singer Billy Idol comes on, his brushcut hair now back from shocking red to peroxide blond, and says "Hi, we're the new signed Generation X, just like the old unsigned Generation X" and his band slam into instant blitzkreig, sending their hardcore fans at the front of the stage into a frenzied pogoing rampage. Bob Andrews builds his wall of merciless metal with a guitar sound harder, more metallic than almost any around. He carries the music of the band while Billy, oozing teen charisma, carries the

BILLY IDOL OF GENERATION X

performance, always with a smile round the corners of his sneer, rubbing saliva from his lips with the back of his right hand, punching the air in classic gestures of aggro, and cracking the microphone lead whip-style with his free hand.

Billy Idol is one of those rare performers who are 50% glamour and 50% aggro, and who work by sheer dazzle. Rock performance is almost always narcissistic, exhibitionistic and chauvinistic, but only a few can make credible those dazzling moments of total self-infatuation, and those few have to look good, move well and be secure in the knowledge that they look good and move well, so that they can siphon the energy feedback from the audience and sustain their sparkle from moment to impossible moment.

In other words, Generation X are a performance band.

So far, so good: the flashiest punk band around come on looking young and pretty and have played some exciting high-energy rock & roll, and the kids have loved it. A mass of crazed punks at the front of the stage are holding onto each others' lapels or shirts judo-style and going apeshit. How they avoid butting each other I will never know. (A week or two later at a Squeeze gig at Dingwalls I see a kid reel away from his mate, eyes flooded, holding his nose, and collapse onto the monitors. In a couple of minutes, though, he was back grinning and leaping about.)

Suddenly, the audience start throwing a large supermarket trolley about in mid-air, while the band are still playing. Where did it come from? A big wire basket in a stainless steel frame with steel handlebars and hard rubber wheels is not part of the furniture of The Vortex, and it's four feet long, so it didn't come in in anybody's handbag.

A lunatic kid stands in the basket and willing, crazy hands hoist him up so he is swaying wildly in front of the stage, a yard from Billy Idol's face, holding onto the light fittings on the low ceiling. He falls out, gets back in, falls out again, gets back in again, and falls out for a third time with the band still playing (but chaotically, losing concentration, and spoiling the number) and then another guy gets in and is hoisted up but he falls out as well. Then a girl who looks drunk gets in. There is always some tomboy who wants to have a go, and with the band playing louder and faster than ever, and Billy looking anxious and slightly upstaged, the girl loses her balance and suddenly does a backward kamikaze dive out of the basket.

At this moment, I am at the side of the stage, and as she is in mid-air, facing me, I can see the expression on her face, an expression of terror. She thinks she is about to die. As some punks dive out of the way, others leap forward to catch her before she hits the floor head first. Tragedy is inches away: fractured skull, tabloids front-paging "NEW PUNK ATROCITY, GLC CLOSE VORTEX," and Generation X relegated to a tour of Norwegian fishing villages.

The line between fun and danger has been crossed. People watched these few minutes of vivid, spontaneous theatre helplessly, with a mixture of amusement and horror. As usual the security goons are nowhere to be seen when they are needed most.

It should be stressed, however, that most punk behaviour is good clean fun. Between bands they drank, listened to the reggae on the disco, talked, bummed cigarettes off each other, bummed lights off each other, threw beer on each other, lobbed ice-cubes at each other, sat on each other, tickled each other, and larked around harmlessly. It was no surprise to see that 15-year-old punkettes were drinking vodka and tonics at the same alarming rate that 15-year-old girls anywhere drink vodka and tonics. Mostly the kids were just fooling around with their friends, not offending strangers. When Generation X came on I stood on a small circular table to get a better view, and two punks stood on it with me, but there was no hassle or obnoxiousness.

There are a few kids with "CHELSEA F.C." tattooed on their arms, but as far as I can see, none with Generation X tattoos. But it's coming. There are plenty of Billy Idol lookalikes in the audience. So far, the band have yet to make a wrong move. They are being skilfully managed by my old pal, Stewart Joseph. With The Clash involved only in confrontations and not playing gigs, and The Sex Pistols only playing a short mini-tour of Europe, Generation X have taken over the summer by default. A week earlier The Jam finished their first headline tour, just as the second single was charting, with a gig at the Hammersmith Odeon where they sold about 3000 tickets, so it looked full. Reports varied. Some said it was a fiasco, others said it was OK, pogoing, lots of encores. The point is this: once you play The Odeon, you can't go back to clubs.

Generation X draw aother 600 fans on the Tuesday night at The Vortex. On the Friday of the following week they return to The Marquee at the other end of Wardour Street, where they draw another 1000. As I go in, club manager, Uli, is standing in the doorway and says "I only turned 200 away. I turned 500 away last time."

Melody Maker's reporter Ian Birch was at the supermarket trolley gig, and *Melody Maker* give Gen X their first front page that week, a huge and somewhat unflattering action pic of Billy. It may be that another 500 punks would have come, but knew they were never going to get in.

The band do a short, sloppy set, but such is their success it hardly matters. The whole ambience of the gig is a curious mixture. When I walk in, the sound is so feeble, I figure it must be the support band. During the set several plastic pint pots are thrown at the stage, usually hitting a pogoing punk on the head and ricocheting over Billy's shoulder into the cymbals.

Of course, the music is sloppy for all the usual reasons. When a group is up-and-coming and trying to get a deal, the only thing they have to think about is doing a good gig and going down well. As soon as they sign the deal they are in the record company offices listening to rough mixes, looking at schedules, chatting up the secretaries, raiding the refrigerators, wanking over photographs of themselves, and generally being distracted from the job in hand. When they get to the gig, the dressing room is chocabloc with admirers old and new. For a while, they have the illusion they have made it, when in fact the real work has hardly even started.

Still, this is Generation X's moment, and they are enjoying it. They have had the front cover of *Melody Maker* and put 1000 fans into The Marquee without even having a record out.

⊚?"*!⊚ Talking About The Pistols !"⊚?*₹!⊚

The phone rang again.
"Whaddya think of the Pistols breaking up?"
"Don't believe it, it's another stunt."
"No, it's true. Official. Kaput."
"What happened?"
"Too much too soon. San Francisco wasn't ready for them. They had to play to 5000 people at Winterland and couldn't deliver. It was sold out a week in advance, with 3000 turned away. I'm sure their agent knew they were famous enough to fill it. And he could earn more commission on a middle-level hall."
"Yeah, but it's better to play to the people that are not there. A small venue would have been more exciting."
"Maybe it was down to the legend of Bill Graham?"
"The heaviest promoter ever?"
"Yeah, when Bill offers you a date, you take it."
"Because you might need him on the next tour?"
"Yes, and if you play hard to get he won't forget."
"They should have stuck to clubs, punk strongholds."
"If Winterland was a bad management decision it's the first blunder McLaren has made in all this time. You've got to remember that they are the only punk band that sells records."
"And Johnny Rotten's the only clever boy with charisma."
"Who owns the name?"
"Malcolm I would think."
"He's got it registered at the Board of Trade?"
"Yeah, someone as sharp as him isn't going to fuck up on an essential detail like that."
"Did you know that they turned down a big TV show which Elvis Costello did instead and caused a sensation?"
"Yeah, that's what they should have done. Do a bit of TV and a mini-tour, hope to get banned, tell reporters 'We're outlaws, they won't let us play!' and then do a guerrilla tour, popping up unannounced. Build up mystique by scarcity."
"Can you do that in USA, it's so big?"
"I dunno, but I wonder if British punk is gonna travel."
"You mean it's just occupational therapy for British teenagers?"
"Yeah, it's got a social content which just won't be understood abroad, especially in affluent countries."
"Are you saying Malcolm won't crack America?"
"Who knows? It's early days yet. Do you think the other two got fed up with John and Sid and Malcolm getting all the press?"
"No, they're pretty normal musicians, Steve and Paul."
"Hanging out in Rio with Ronnie Biggs isn't that normal!"
"What a brainwave! Who else would have thought of that but Malcolm McLaren? Biggs the train robber in exile in Brazil. A natural for front pages."
"What will happen next?"
"Pistols to reform? Rumours?"
"It's over, says spokesman for Glitterbest."
"They're very loyal Malcolm's staff, they all tell the same story, all the time, it's marvellous."
"Anyday now he will say they've offered him Beatles-scale money. A million dollars to reform and do one song live on satellite TV."
"Live from the 100 Club!"
"Where else?"
"Full circle. What used to take 18 years now takes 18 months."
"More like 18 minutes. Howard Devoto got the front page of *Melody Maker* after only eleven gigs."
"Who's Howard Devoto?"
"Last week's enigma."
"What is it in February then?"
"Maybe the Rich Kids. Bass player kicked out of Pistols 'cos he likes Beatles too much, has smash with new group. He was the songwriter in the band. He doesn't need controversy."
"You can't hum a controversy on the way to work."
"Punks don't go to work."
"The Rich Kids aren't punk, they're New Wave."
"When I hear something new, I'll wave."
"Why don't Malcolm and John do the *Russell Harty* show?"
"A talk show wouldn't add to their myth. They're already legends in their own lifetimes."
"Both are already acting as if they have been famous for ten years."

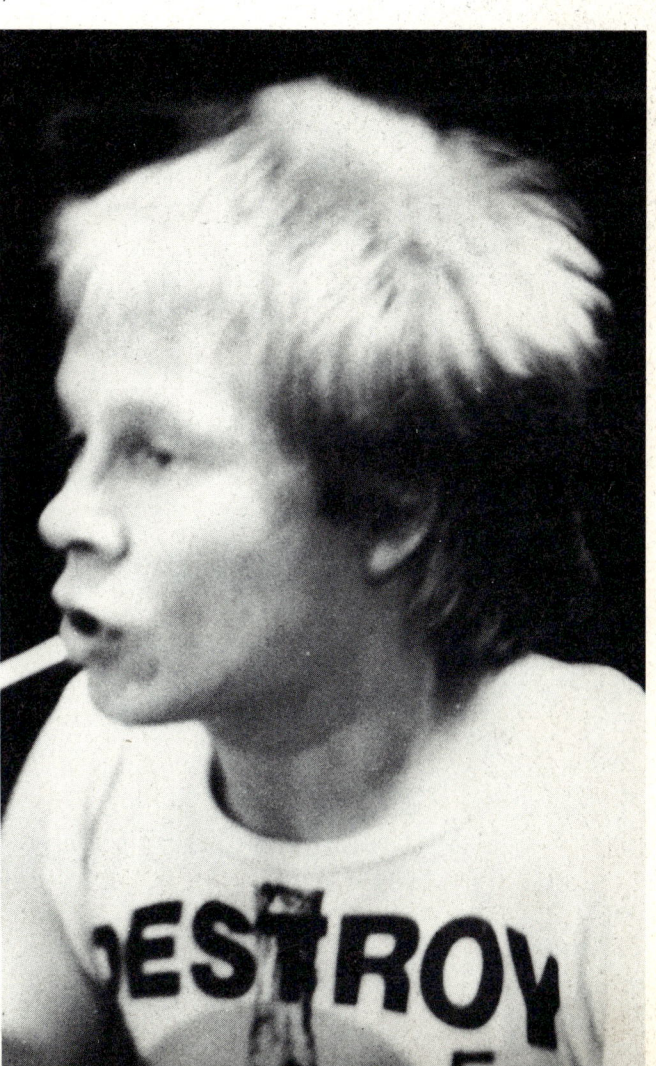

PAUL COOK

"The best move now is no move."
"Exactly."
"Let press speculation build a bit."
"Yeah, a few stories along the lines of 'Do Malcolm and Johnny *really* hate each other'."
"Or do they claim to, just because it's good copy."
"The Sex Pistols aren't a group, they're a serial."
"Controversy Street, based on an original idea by Malcolm McLaren."
"Test-marketed by the New York Dolls."
"Malcolm must have loads of unreleased tapes and miles of celluloid in the can."
"He could sell the live tapes to American bootleggers."
"Then Warner Bros could prosecute Pistols tape pirates."
"BOOTLEG PROBE INJUNCTION ARREST SCANDAL!"
"Story follows story."
"It's self-perpetuating."
"All serials are."
"Especially in America where people are greedy for whatever's next and don't worry about details like 'Is it any good', or 'Does it make sense?'"
"Malcolm is very hip compared to most managers."
"Right, he'll never release the definitive Pistols film."
"It would be self-defeating."
"It would end discussion."
"It would circumscribe them, which is the last thing he wants."
"Do we expect to see Sex Pistols Mark 3 in March?"
"With Steve and Paul and a new bass player?"
"Captain Sensible of The Damned, he's fearless."
"Yeah, but he's been offered it once already."
"And he keeps taking his trousers off in people's offices."
"That can get a bit boring."
"New bass player and straight back to conquer USA!"
"As Oscar Wilde said, it's not a question of will the playing be a success, it's a question of will the audience be a success."
"Oscar was the first punk."
"And if Oscar had been managing the band he would have sacked Sid before they went and cracked America first time."
"Well, you can't win 'em all."
"No, but you can go for 'em all."
"You always say that."
"Talk to you tomorrow."
"Right! Bye."

Gary Numan's Modern World

The hippy dream was one of escape. It was all about going up country and dropping out and turning on and going to San Francisco with flowers in your hair. It was idealistic, contemplative, sometimes mystical. Above all, it was a rejection of urban consumer culture.

The Grateful Dead were a folk-blues band, not a rock band. Most of the West Coast groups had beginnings in folky, acoustic music. If you were stoned enough and listening to Crosby Stills and Nash it was easy to believe that their fabulous blend of voices actually meant something. The harmony of the universe, maybe.

Joni Mitchell was a hip princess who sang "They paved paradise, put up a parking lot, they took all the trees, put 'em in a tree museum, charged the people a dollar and a half just to see 'em."

Later, the main ethic in pop music was to be the acceptance and celebration of the modern world. From the moment in September 1969 when we first heard those magic words "Ground control to Major Tom", the pop cosmos had changed. The first line of *Space Oddity* was a signal for the Seventies to begin, and David Bowie became the premier influence on young songwriters.

Bowie was topical and technological, a chameleon who was everywhere and nowhere, a workaholic who turned himself into a legend by hopping from *Life On Mars*, to plastic soul, to pin-up pics with Twiggy, to a film with Nick Roeg, to recording with Eno in Berlin, to acting in a stage play on Broadway.

Much that came later was Bowiestream. There was Ultravox, John Foxx, Spandau Ballet and of course the most blatant Bowie imitator of all, Gary Numan. As a teenage Bowie fan himself, Gary Webb had the market well sussed. A lonely youth, Gary went out driving in his car and thinking about how there was now all this acceptance of synthesiser pop but no showmanship. He realised that David Bowie had created a demand, then taken away the supply.

The public was ready for a synthesiser star. Gary bought some eyeliner and practised his reptilian sneer and soon had three LPs in the Top Twenty simultaneously, and two Number One singles under the belt of his space-cadet uniform. His name change was perfect. No name could have been better. Gary had maximum working class karma, and Numan had a hint of novelty and futurism.

At first his group was called Tubeway Army. They played music which was ultra-simplistic and ultra-robotic, and Gary sang like a Dalek: songs of loneliness, frustration and alienation. Very remote and computerised. Tubeway Army swiftly catapulted ahead of all the other synthesiser bands of the time.

For teenagers the actual scientific conquest of space was something they had seen on the television news, and grown up with. Landing on the moon was no longer a fantasy but an event of modern life, almost like getting on a bus or playing a cassette. Gary Numan was cute, but weird, and the kids could believe he was a lost young man, a victim wandering and confused in an alien environment. Gary looked slightly strange, just otherworldly enough. It did not matter that he lacked the wit and worldliness of Bowie, since most of his fans were only twelve years old. Gary Numan had instant image, instant sound, and instant success.

At his farewell concerts at Wembley Arena in April 1981 he played to almost 30,000 fans with a typical stage production which simulated the spectacular spaceship landing from the blockbuster movie *Close Encounters Of The Third Kind*. The set had many huge coloured panels which used 72 sheets of Perspex, and there were hydraulic lifts, radio-controlled robots, three tons of lighting equipment, a radio-controlled car for the encore, and a film of pilot Gary flying his own twin-engined jet above Hampshire. Space was no longer science fiction. It had become cabaret for suburban teenagers.

His two live compilation albums *Living Ornaments '79* and *Living Ornaments '80* were available as a boxed set for a limited period of a month (a smart marketing gimmick) and they duly rocketed to No.2 in the charts, tucking in behind the ever-present *Kings Of The Wild Frontier* by Adam and the Ants.

THE ROUGH EDGES OF THE POLICE

The key characteristic of British groups is their rough edges. This roughness helped bring international acclaim to The Rolling Stones, Free, Joe Cocker, Led Zeppelin and Rod Stewart, among others. Onstage they have a kind of boisterous charm which foreigners find appealing, and in the studio they manage to keep some of that raunchy edge, even when they are spending months rather than days recording, and using sophisticated equipment, which tends to make everything sound smooth.

The Stones album *Some Girls* was recorded in a 16-track rehearsal studio in Paris and was a return to their raw R&B roots. It was raucous body music. *Respectable* had locomotive propulsion. Jagger's juggernaut was rolling again, and *Miss You* had superloud bass drum and even a harmonica. *Some Girls* was a giant comeback album, which sold an astonishing 14 million worldwide.

The Keith Richard-Mick Jagger creative process is one which is typical of guitar groups. Keith writes the music and gives Mick a cassette of a new song, and the singer writes lyrics which fit the sound and feel of the track, so that the roughness is retained. Groups where the lyrics are written first often tend to be keyboard-oriented groups: Traffic, Procol Harum, Elton John.

The Police continue the British tradition of rough edges. Not being punks in 1976, they couldn't get gigs, and after they had replaced original guitarist Henri Padovani, who had been playing for 15 minutes, with Andy Summers, who had been playing for 15 years, their rehearsals started to sound more interesting. They jammed and evolved a couple of songs in the reggae style. They were not a wall-of-sound trio but a sparse, empty-sounding trio with music based around riff and poppy lyrics.

Although they did not know it, the market was ready for them. There is nothing stronger than an idea whose time has come, and it was the moment for a white man to sing reggae-influenced pop.

Sting was the voice and *Roxanne* was the song. *Roxanne* sounds like a group playing rather than a group making a record. It is bare and raw and rough as a badger's arse. The singer is a hero who saves souls. "You don't have to sell your body through the night," he sings, "My mind is made up, you don't have to put on the red light."

Typically, the BBC buried *Roxanne* when it was first released just as they had buried *Sultans Of Swing*. Like Dire Straits, The Police broke abroad before they were accepted in Britain. *So Lonely* sounds live, like a group who have been playing for two hours and are lurching, slapping and wailing through their third encore and it is this ragged quality, this pain, this sense of struggle which makes Sting's vocal persona so affecting. His yearning and longing sound believable as he sings "in this desert that I call my soul, I always play the starring role."

As it worked out, The Police's early career was untypical. What usually happens is that a group plays some gigs for a few months, gets a reputation, signs a record contract and is put into an expensive studio for a short time with a producer approved by the record company. The Police were put into a cheap studio for a longer time with an engineer. They played and told him what they wanted. They were not compromised by a producer who may have had preconceived ideas about what sells, or how they should record, or what worked well for him the last time he produced a similar group.

So the sound of the first two Police albums is diabolical, but their style comes over because they are able to play and sing uninhibitedly. *Outlandos D'Amour* and *Regatta de Blanc* do not sound perfect, which is sometimes an advantage, since when you sound perfect you invariably sound like someone else.

The Police is good pop loosely played. Where so many other songwriters are either juvenile or parochial or descriptive, Sting is universal. Other groups all listen to phone-in radio shows. They have all missed the last bus home. They are all in love with the girl at the record store check-out desk. They are all losers. They do not transcend, they just listen and complain. There are hundreds of groups guilty of this but the Members are a typical example. The Members were the first group to do suburban reggaes. It was a bright idea, but it was the only idea they ever had: "Same old boring Sunday morning, old man's out washing the car, Mum's in the kitchen…

At this point my ears switch off. I don't want to hear about his brother having a bath, his sister doing something else. Who cares? When I hear "This is the sound of the suburbs!" I shout at the radio "Stop wanking! Get a day job!"

On the other hand Sting writes about feelings: Walkin' back from your place, walkin' on the moon, bed's too big without you, I can't sleep with your memory, no-one's knocked on my door for a thousand years or more, I'll send an S.O.S. to the world, I hope that someone gets my message in a bottle." This kind of imagery is pure Carole King, classic pop. You just know that when this old world is getting him down, Sting goes up on the roof.

Sting writes about the right things, where The Members and groups like them always write about the wrong things. Sting says a lot in one line. The first line of one of his smash hits is: "Young teacher, the subject of schoolgirl fantasy." Schoolgirls have been standing too close to the teacher for a long time. The musical skill of The Police's song-construction is often ignored by critics who slag off their lyrics as bland and banal. *Message In a Bottle* has a sequence of three hooks which made it one of the catchiest singles ever to reach Number One.

And all over the world in 1980 when teenagers met and were trying to suss each other out, one of the first questions they asked each other was "Do you like The Police?" And the kids would have to figure out whether it was hip to admit you liked them, or hip to say you didn't like them even if you did, or cool to say you liked them even if you loathed them.

CHRIS THOMAS GETS THE VOCAL PERFORMANCE

Personality.

In his wonderfully wise and witty book, *How To Have A Lifestyle*, Quentin Crisp says "Outside of natural catastrophes, the greatest power on earth is personality."

In a rock group most of the personality comes from the singer. When a group is recorded by a producer, he often gives them his sound, rather than pursues their sound, so he is often taking personality out when he should be leaving it in, or creating it. When Chris Thomas first took The Sex Pistols into the studio there were many whispers. How is it going? Everyone wanted to know. The word filtered back: "Chris thinks the band are brilliant, but the singer can't sing. If he could sing, they'd be the new Stones."

Johnny Rotten can't sing, but he has a way of delivering a lyric which is hard to ignore, and Chris Thomas had the audacity to turn a weakness into a strength. He encouraged Rotten to be as extreme as possible. *Never Mind The Bollocks* is a classic because the singer's performance is so sustained. A raging young punk snarls and sneers through eleven songs and never lets up. He is totally uncompromising. The anger and intensity of his vocals are somehow, miraculously, equal to the impact of Steve Jones's skullbusting guitar.

"I'm a lazy sod, I'm a lazy sod, I'm so layzeeargh!" he screams. "I am an anti-Christ, I wanna destroy" he snarls on *Anarchy*. Rotten cackles and laughs like a demon. "We're so pretty, oh so pretty ...VACANT !!!! " he yells, "And we don't care!" There is no holding back: "She had an abortion" he screams, "You're just a pile of shit." He chats and whines and bawls his way through the grinding *Submission* and closes the track with a bronchial cough.

The anger of a raw, young group is brought into perfect focus by the craftsmanship of Chris Thomas, and his brilliant engineer Bill Price. They made the Pistols sound powerful, and every other punk record of the time sounded feeble and amateurish, by comparison. Of course for a time punks wanted to sound amateurish, but that was just a phase. Ultimately recording is a medium of precision and sounding cheap and messy was a fad. Power chords are layered to build the most dynamic sound possible. The Steve Jones-Bill Price guitar sound is among the angriest in the whole history of rock & roll, but in the end it is the Chris Thomas-Johnny Rotten vocal persona, the cumulative impact of the eleven performances on those eleven songs, which makes *Bollocks* the definitive punk masterpiece. Chris Thomas also made The Pretenders sound different to any other group. Sure, Chrissie Hynde has a great voice, but hundreds of girls have great voices. It is what Chris Thomas gets her to do with her voice that makes the album, and makes the group. She did not sing like that when Nick Lowe produced her. Thomas distilled the group's playing to make them sound distinctive and, on side two, creates an instrumental canvas upon which Chrissie can stretch out, mumble, complain, whisper, make remarks, plead, scream, talk to herself and generally create her vocal personality.

"I'm very superficial, I hate anything official," she confides on *Private Life* and as the track purrs along she warns that "Your sexlife complications are not my fascinations". The two loud and nasty guitar solos set back in the mix, provide nicely melodramatic punctuation before the song finishes, and the side chugs into the powerful, lazy and truly unusual *Brass In Pocket* Chrissie Hynde is the first woman to sing rock. Ever. Other girls and women have either shouted, or sung pop.

A producer is obviously limited by the songs but Chris Thomas can work wonders with weak material which is why he gets 4% of an album and only does two projects a year. And even Chris can't make *Lovers of Today* into a song. It is just a gentle jam with lyrics, crescendoes and a marvellously vague fade. He makes it into good filler. His wonderfully subtle mixing and programming make Side Two of The Pretenders debut into something more lastingly listenable than anything The Police have done so far, despite the fact that Stewart and Sting and Andy are much better players.

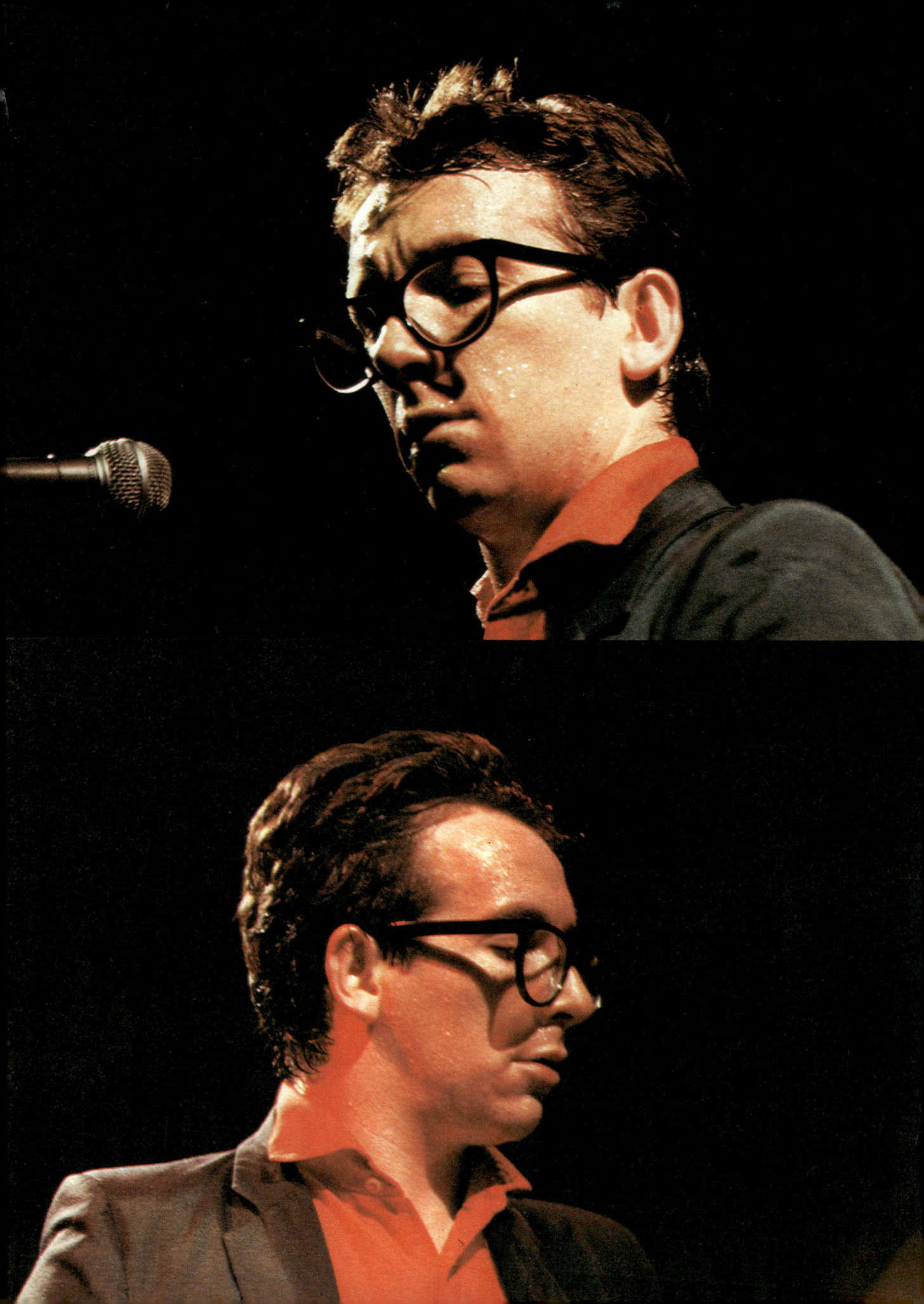

ELVIS
AT THE DOMINION

The bombscare is my first bombscare at a rock concert. Everyone is told to leave so that the cinema, The Dominion in Tottenham Court Rd, can be searched. We adjourn to a nearby coffee bar. It is of course, a false alarm and the ticketless perpetrators no doubt cruise in with the returning crush. If the/a hoaxer rings up next time the manager should say, "Look, if you are that desperate to see Elvis Costello we'll give you a ticket, then at least we can start the show on time."

As before, four musicians run onstage. The image is the same: short hair, tinted shades, ties, tight-bottomed trousers. Costello is in red winklepickers and an Italian suit. They slam into *What's So Funny About Peace, Love And Understanding?* and then two more fast numbers before he says "Good evening!" The music is slick, racy, pacy and belligerent. They do a new song *Accident*, something which sounds good but I can't hear the words, and they open out *Watching The Detectives* with a monologue and a jam and make it a centrepiece, but they play it a shade too early in the set. *Lipstick Vogue* doesn't hold my attention but I do get into *This Year's Girl* because it is like the album but louder and faster. In fact, the whole concert is like the album but louder and faster.

The Attractions ensemble sound gets fire from the drums, propulsion from the bass, and colour from the keyboards but drummer Pete Thomas is too rocky and there are too many repetitious crescendoes and too many numbers sound the same. Generally the band play against Elvis, not with him. They don't showcase his persona or his voice or his songs. Tall guitarist Martin Belmont joins them for an encore of *Pump It Up*, which is predicably raucous.

Elvis Costello and the Attractions have a strange approach to a big stage. They set up their gear as if they are playing a youth club, with the amps clustered centrestage round a drum kit barely raised on a shallow rostrum. Perversely, they seem to want to be a Sixties beat group. They can sell out seven nights at The Dominion but they can't even fill the stage.

Right now, in 1978, I care about Elvis Costello more than any other rock artist. The songs on *This Year's Model* have kept me buzzing for months and I must have listened to it more than any album since Bob Marley's *Natty Dread*. I have looked forward to this concert for months. During the week I have said (1) I do not think he can cut it as a concert act and (2) If he is good, it will mean a lot to me. I was ready to be thrilled and liberated but he did not make my heart beat faster, or even applaud once. Nothing he played, sang or did could move me. I listened, looked and waited but the moment never came and now the Mrs is driving me home and I hear myself say "I'm surprised he didn't do *Alison*" and she says "But he did do *Alison*," which shows how much of my attention he was commanding.

Even more worrying, he seems to have mellowed. I want him to maintain his intense personality. Stick to your guns, kid! You're right! Life is a blandout! We need your spleen, we need your abrasive intelligence, mocking our dull conventions and expectations! You are in danger of losing the thing we love you for!

Personality, after all, begins at the point where one man plays a role no other man can play. Still, on the other hand, he has to accept he is in showbiz. Maybe tomorrow he will be at a party and some mutual acquaintance will say "Elvis, I want you to meet Paul McCartney." What is he gonna do? Spit on Paul's outstretched hand?

On the way home through Camden Town we drop in to The Electric Ballroom to see Generation X, and it turns out to be the end of Generation X, or at least the beginning of the end. We watch the last three numbers. The hall is half empty. It's a shambles. I cannot believe people are still throwing beer and plastic glasses. It is the first time I have ever seen them not get an encore. Blond-mopped Billy and the boys walk off to the sound of their own feet.

I turn round to talk to Eddy and see Johnny Rotten standing behind her. I look again and realise that this kid is only 17 or 18 and looks just like the current Public Image poster of Johnny. Only a very young Rotten lookalike would be seen dead at a Generation X gig this late in the game.

Soon after this, Costello chatted with DJ Nicky Horne on London's Capital Radio, just after the release of his third album *Armed Forces*. He played a Chas and Dave song *One Thing And Another* for Ian Dury to celebrate Ian's No. 1 with *Rhythm Stick*, although admitting that he has had his differences with Dury in the past. He then played a really whacky track with mildly strolling piano and spacey guitar and the rambling verbals of the inimitable John Cooper Clarke: "Make a date with the brassy brides of Britain, the altogether ruder reader's wives, who put down their needles and their knitting at the doorways to our dismal daily lives, the Fablon top scenarios of passion, nipples peek through holes in leatherette, they seem to be saying in their fashion 'I'm freezing Charlie, have you finished yet?', Cold flesh the colour of potatoes in an Instamatic living room of sin, all the required apparatus, too bad they couldn't fit her head in. . . ."

It was strange to hear the seductively smooth commercials alternating with the unseductive, unsmooth Costello and his unsettling record choices. He certainly wasn't trying to anaesthetize the way we feel on this radio-radio show. He was annoying, but playfully self-aware: "This is Elvis Costello on 194, playin' the records and irritatin' ya . . ."

He played *I'm Your Man* by Richard Hell and the Voidoids and told us that if we didn't go out and buy it there must be something wrong with our ears. I thought it sounded like early Stones but not so good. I must have something wrong with my ears. He also played a disgustingly incoherent Clash track from *Give 'Em Enough Rope*, but redeemed himself with John Lennon's *Instant Karma*, a great record, if not a great song.

NE 2-TONE 2-T

Bandleader Jerry Dammers had the bright idea of starting a movement rather than just starting a group.
After experimenting with a mixture of punk and reggae, Jerry's Coventry-based Specials stormed London with a fusion of punk and ska, playing a lot of covers. Their indie single *Gangsters* stole the hook phrase from the mid-Sixties hit *Al Capone* by Prince Buster and sold steadily on the strength of the group's live appearances. It had an instrumental B-side by The Selecter, another Coventry band who were friends of The Specials.
Several record companies were interested, including CBS, but CBS were too corporate and too far removed from the street to realise the value of giving The Specials their own label, so Jerry signed with Chrysalis who agreed to let him release a few singles by his mates on his own 2-Tone label. Thus unknown groups such as Madness and The Beat released their first singles on 2-Tone, and a music/fashion movement was financed and marketed nationally and, later, internationally.
Madness were a North London group who took their name from a Prince Buster song and they signed to Stiff and rushed their first album in order to get it out at the same time as The Specials. Being a performance band rather than a music band they were exactly the kind of group who should not rush an album. Suggsy's vocals are engaging but one-dimensional and *One Step Beyond* was typical Stiff product: lively, but under-produced, pub-rock with a ska beat. They developed promisingly and soon had eight straight hits.
The Beat's version of *Tears Of A Clown* was the best-played and best-produced of the early 2-Tone singles and following the example of The Specials they signed to Arista, a deal which allowed them to release five singles a year on their own Go-Feet label. They then released no records other than their own and gave the lame excuse that they were on the road all the time and did not have a chance to see other bands.
Their debut album *I Just Can't Stop It,* was by far the best of the bunch, with Bob Sargeant's sharp production holding all the elements in balance. The music was accessible but not bland, and a reminder that The Beat are not only better players than Madness and The Specials, but also much better singers. They have wide appeal. Girls like the two singers because they are good-looking. Blacks like the reggae element, and punks like the fast numbers such as *Click Click,* with its churning, rushing, galloping excitement.
UB40, another West Midlands group, took their name from the unemployment benefit form and used the form as their album packaging concept for *Signing Off.* The music has a magic mood, soothing and seducing, gliding painlessly from track to track. There is no warmer groove anywhere, and the political lyrics are slurred, blurred and indistinct, with only the occasional phrase like "ivory madonna" and "Tyler is guilty" jumping out on a cursory first listen.
Generally, the 2-Tone wave of groups mix entertainment and social content, but in varying degrees. Madness are fun. The

MADNESS

Specials are fun with an edge. UB40 are mood massage with an edge, and The Beat are UB40 with pop charisma. I like fun with an edge. All fun is no fun, and all edge is no fun either, which is why I hate the Joy Division school of A-level angst.

I first saw The Specials at the Lyceum, bottom of the bill to the Gang Of Four, and they were dreadful. Headlining the Hammersmith Palais after their second album, they were still dreadful. No amount of high-energy showmanship could prevent me from noticing that there was no groove. At The Lyceum I could not believe that a sevenpiece group could make such a thin sound, or that they had no sax player. How could a sevenpiece ska band not have a saxaphone? They could not sing, they had no material, the sound was appalling, and they never hit a groove, let alone sustained a groove.

As usual, the audience was by far the best part of the show. The bopping skinheads were a sight for sore eyes, and I finally figured out why skinheads have tattoos. To distinguish the boys from the girls. When they the boys started wearing earrings and the girls went butch with braces and bovverboots it was hard to tell the difference, so the boys got tattoos. I caught Madness on a five group bill headlined by the Secret Affair at the peak of the mod revival, and the audience was better rehearsed than the band. Madness at the time were a travelling party machine for extrovert skinheads.

Late one night on the tube a couple of skinhead girls chat me up on the tube and we have a hilarious conversation, most of

which I have now forgotten. The taller of the two is about 18 and she is loud and lively and wears jeans, boots, white T-shirt and braces and her opening line is "Have you ever travelled on the tube before?" to which I replied "Have you ever been impertinent before?" and they giggled and said "What's impertinent mean?" and I said "Cheeky!" I thought they were a lot of fun, didn't seem to care about anything, and that if I was in a group, they were the sort of fans I would like to have. They are the sort who are so keen to participate in a concert that their nutty dancing begins two seconds before the group starts to play the first number.

Punks always tell me there is no such thing as punk violence, there is only skinhead violence. It is true that a lot of these lads have given lots of people a good kicking and smashed many a windscreen during Easter rampages through seaside towns, but I often find it hard to consider them a threat to society. I keep thinking of the night a junior skin was trying to blag his way to Dingwalls one night when I arrived for a Bodysnatcher's gig. The lad was about 15 and I arrived at the box-office in time to hear him say to the girl behind the window: "'Course I'm old enough, I drive for the Post Office, I haven't got my license wiv me! Oh come on let me in! You let me in two weeks ago, Saturday night, three quid, I can't remember what band it was!" and he was so cuddly I wanted to scoop him up and hide him under my jacket and smuggle him in so that when the disco played *The Last Train To Skaville* he could have hopped about happily with his mates.

THE SPECIALS IN NEW YORK

New York Notes

The Slits at the Ritz

The Ritz is an almost square balconied ballroom, smaller than London's Lyceum but bigger than the Electric. There are three tiers of casual seating on the left, and more seating on the far side. The whole of the back wall is taken up by a second stage containing the DJ, the sound mixer and the lighting crews. The sightlines and soundlines are great. It is the biggest small rock room I have ever seen, and by far the best.

In London all the gigs are in rooms which are the wrong size or shape. The Music Machine is a converted radio theatre. Dingwalls is a tunnel. The Venue is a half-converted cinema. The Hope is a sweaty cellar. The Nashville is a big old-fashioned pub room with the stage in an awkward corner. They are all horrible gigs to play and lousy places to see a band. The Marquee is still our only decent rock club.

I am thrilled with The Ritz. The ambience is great. It has that elusive balance which Americans create so professionally, the right blend of darkness and light, of community and privacy, of colour and black and white. The volume level is crucial: it must be loud enough to be exciting but not too loud to prevent conversation. The audience is scruffier than I expected. There are a few urchin punks and Slits lookalikes. There are maybe 1200 people here, and maybe most of them are expecting some kind of rasta-feminist freak show, rather than music from London's original female punks.

After three numbers by The Slits I find myself wishing they would do covers. Mostly they are a noisy mass of percussion and wailing. They apparently profess to despise conventional song structures and here they sound like party time in the parrot house. They have almost no material but they are clearly the kind of group to whom you tend to give the benefit of the doubt. Maybe I caught 'em on a bad night, you think, I'll go and check them out again, see if they have improved.

In fact, Ari is just not a good rhythm singer. It's as simple as that. When she takes her hat off we see that it's not a hat but a striped scarf which she knots in her hair making her dreadlocks stick up vertically. Ari is the Vanessa Redgrave of punk. The Slits may be messy and musically vague but they wear great hats. The three girls are helped out by three guys on drums, guitar and assorted keyboards/trumpet. *Typical Girls* burps along but never really hits a groove. I have the feeling that it's not so much that they can't play, so much as they don't rehearse enough. For the encore they do a spacey version of *I Heard It Through The Grapevine,* which is good but it stops too soon and they dash off again.

THE SLITS (LEFT AND ABOVE)

Yes, as a late night's bite of the Big Apple, I like The Ritz. When it's 2.30 a.m. and the dreamlazy reggae is rolling over you and your feet submerge in the mess of fag ends and melting ice cubes and men are kissing men and lesbian punkettes are swirling wildly and sleazoid punk lovers are dancing with erotic abandon and your nerves are jangled by the abrasive, blanket attack of Public Image and the gaunt visage of chairman Johnny is staring down from the giant video screen. The Ritz is the only place to be.

As we leave the leather jacketed youth who opened up earlier is standing on the stairs.

"What time do you close?" I ask.

"4 o'clock, sir!"

I love that "sir." Service! Have a nice day! Have a punky all-nighter! New York is by far the best place to see an English group, with good facilities and staff like this guy. You would never get the staff of The Marquee or The Rock Garden calling you "sir" in a million years.

Next day, trying to digest the evening, I decide that The Slits are a sham and a shambles. They are a problem band who have had about 20 managers already. It is not Ari's fault she is a spoiled rich kid, who never had any discipline from her German banker father, because her parents were estranged and her young Mum was one of the original Kensington punk liggers when her darling daughter was a spiky sixteen. But The Slits have been an endearing oddity for too long. They should pack up or own up. If they own up, they should do some good songs by Sting or Costello or someone, and if they are hung up on black songwriters, they should record some black songs because, heaven knows, there are plenty of good black writers who could use the royalties.

ARI OF THE SLITS

Talkadelic Heads at Radio City

The palatial Art Deco foyer of Radio City is more exciting than most groups. I'm scared they're gonna charge me again to go inside the theatre. The whole of this huge building is carpeted wall-to-wall, so the ambience is soft, comfortable, almost domestic, as if the hall is a home-from-home for 6,000 people a night.

The record playing as we find our seats is by Gary Numan, confirming my theory that every record finds its level and function eventually. Gary Numan is perfect muzak to find your seats by.

Steel Pulse come on and start playing and my Mrs says "It's a good solid sound" and I recall that the last time I saw this group was at The Vortex in 1977 where the entire floor space of the club is smaller than the stage of Radio City.

In UK it has become hip to slag Steel Pulse as the Abba of reggae but here they remind me of War: a tight professionally programmed show which makes the most of some flimsy material. They play more authoritatively than War, laying down a chunky and funky groove. As one song ends gradually, they slowly collapse down onto the stage, knelling like crumpled puppets as the drummer hits a final cymbal and somehow it's not corny, just fun, a good moment.

There are cheers and roars as five figures dash onstage and grab their guitars. Blonde Tina Weymouth looks Twiggyish in a black Sixties mini-dress and cherry pink tights. David Byrne is typically minimal in his black trousers and mauve shirt. Sartorially, for the thin black duke, less is more.

Talking Heads are the local heroes here, and when they kick off, they kick ass: the huge hall is filled with raw sound. *Psychokiller* is an irresistable barrage of rhythm and metallic power, taut sledgehammer funk. It is a devastating and awesome moment. Everyone jumps to their feet. I stop taking notes and surrender to the potent rhythm.

The music is dense, tense, jagged, visceral. For a rock-funk orchestra they are sparse. Eventually they have nine musicians onstage, although most of the time it seems to me that three of the four black musicians are redundant. Only the percussionist adds anything vital. Adrian Belew's feedback excursions make the band sound as if they are motoring through an earthquake. Its hard for a guitarist to make mad noises, much harder than people realise, which is why Belew is a guitarist's guitarist and was valued so highly by Frank Zappa and David Bowie.

Byrne's brainchild has been evolving gradually from a trio to the sophisticated polyrhythmic textures of *Remain In Light*, their fourth album. Talking Heads have material, musicianship, intelligence and a sense of career, and they have fused their new style and sound from head music, drug music and African dance music. They play rock and roll for the mind and body and as we leave during a raw encore of *Take Me To The River* I am convinced that they are by far the most interesting and imaginative major rock group in USA.

Never mind the Pistols here's the mclaren

The film, *The Great Rock And Roll Swindle* is a good laugh. It is raunchy, funny and hip, a gaudy mixture of documentary, cartoons, reconstruction and fantasy, and is finally more of a comedy than a music film. Episodic and jumbled, it romps swiftly through many sequences which are disposable, much that is mere silliness.

That the long-awaited Pistols film should be uneven is no surprise. Though flawed, the film is never dull. It is fast, clever and challenging. It works because it has the courage of its vulgarity. Director Julien Temple has used many comic devices, exploiting the comedy of nudity, the comedy of animation, the comedy of controversy, and the comedy of violence. In the notorious Sid-Vicious-in-Paris sequences the surly, pugnacious Sid shoves a cream cake in the face of a prostitute, sings *My Way* and then shoots the audience. It is carnage as cabaret. Film being what it is and young audiences being what they are, the images of Sid (riding his motorbike, swaggering around a foreign capital in his black leather jacket, and gunning down a load of stuffed shirt parents) have had a powerful effect on kids who are ready to believe that Sid kamikazed for the cause of punk rock. Sid died for punk! This is a new and dangerous myth. Sid Vicious was just a poor dumb lout who couldn't compute what was going on around him and was destroyed by events and by an ugly little American girl who turned him into a junkie. Sid was no musician and no songwriter and he tried to compensate for this by outrageous and escalating acts of self-mutilation.

Although the film tell us nothing we do not already know about the *enfants terrible* who ignited the New Wave explosion, it does, oddly enough, reflect the spirit of The Sex Pistols. This is because Temple is not an outsider but an insider and had worked with the band from the start. His film is uncompromising. it never apologises for its amorality. It forces you to make up your own mind. It asks questions. Was it cruel to con kids into travelling all across England to see their heroes at gigs they never had any intention of playing? Or was it just mischievous fun which kept a nation entertained? Was it profoundly cynical to keep on shooting footage on a bewildered junkie who was always likely to die before the film was even shown?

On a purely documentary level *The Great Rock And Roll Swindle* is dishonest, even irrelevant. McLaren would apparently like us to believe that he had no luck and that every move was planned in advance and that he ingeniously outwitted the record companies. This movie is the testament of a manager's arrogance, a memoir and manifesto from a subversive entrepreneur who did it his way. TGRRS is not The Sex Pistols Story, it is the gospel according to Malcolm McLaren in which a self-styled genius tells How I Invented Punk Rock, How I Made The Deals, How I Got All That Press.

SID SHOOTING THE AUDIENCE

When *The Sex Pistols Story* is made, with Johnny Rotten starring as himself, it should include everything this film leaves out: how and why Glen Matlock left, the arguments and fights. It should chart the process by which they all came to hate each other and how it might have been held together for longer if only Rotten had been willing to do what McLaren wanted him to do, or whether McLaren could have been more amenable to the desires of the band. Even now the level of misinformation surrounding The Pistols is phenomenal. The myths have generated counter-myths. This film will do a lot to re-mythologise them, but very little to set the record straight. Malcolm McLaren did not swindle the record business. EMI did not lose a lot of money on The Pistols. Warners made a profit. Virgin made a fortune. A&M lost money but only because they were too timid to release the single they had already pressed. They could have sold a quarter of a million singles and then sacked the group, or entered more into the spirit of the thing by collaborating with McLaren on a stunt and sold half a million. The notion that McLaren conned the record companies is simply not true, although it suits his scenario in this film to pretend that it is. Around the London record business it is said, however, that Virgin boss Richard Branson has never been the same since he met McLaren.

The main weakness of the film is that there is no footage of Rotten offstage (his solicitors insisted it was all cut, but if John has any sense he should allow it to be re-inserted). The idea of Steve Jones going to see his own film is an inspired one, and beautifully sustained. My second visit to the film is in a week when Ronnie Biggs is in custody in Barbados, having been kidnapped from Brazil by mercenaries, and the papers say that Steve Jones has flown out to the island to see his old mate. This may be true. It may not. Either way, Jones is newsworthy for the first time in two years.

The Swindle is revealing, but not candid. Nowhere does

McLaren mention his crucial borrowings from the New York Dolls, Richard Hell or Situationist theory. He seized the moment, but the film does not explain how he was uniquely placed and uniquely qualified to seize the moment. Someone else might have owned a boutique. Someone else might have been bored by conventional rock and liked the trashiness of The Dolls. But no-one else in 1976 was walking in the wild West End with a vision of how a British version of The Dolls could scare the establishment if only they could have a clever young working class singer who had the bottle to actually say (again and again) "Its just a load of old bastards too scared to change" and "We're the only honest band to hit this planet in ten thousand years."

No-one has actually pointed out that all four original Sex Pistols are alive and well and living in London and invisible. It makes you wonder. Should they have abdicated after only one album? Did The Who break up just because they had a few fists fights in the back of the van? Did the Stones break up because Brian Jones (and later Mick Taylor) was out of his box the whole time. Does Johnny need a good talking to? Do the Fab Four of punk have any right to deprive a generation of a band it wants and needs?

The support film to *Swindle* was *Punk Can Take It*, a 20-minute film about the UK Subs, directed by Julien Temple. The Subs burped and snarled through a film which flattered them and one recalled that in 1977 it was often said that the only person who knows the difference between punk and heavy metal was McLaren. Charlie Harper and the lads are just fast and heavy metal with a red-haired drummer. They play youthnoize. The newsreel commentator describes the dilution and merchandising of the punk message: "What had been a weapon they tried to make a toy." The anti-establishment rebellion is seen as the heroic struggle of an oppressed minority.

YOUR CASSETTE PET

The retail trade has long been a source of resistance to the effective marketing of cassettes by the record companies. Most pre-recorded tapes are black with paper labels and come in transparent plastic boxes, every one the same. As merchandise they are unattractive. Small, hard to display, easy to rip off, retailers find cassettes a nuisance and prefer to cling tenaciously to the old-fashioned LP.

With so few good cassettes available, people made their own, and the industry bitched about the loss of profits and formed committees to see what could be done about home-taping on blank cassettes.

Ever sensitive to sources of record company paranoia, Malcolm McLaren writes a lyric called *C-30, C-60, C-90 Go!* and records it with his new protégés Bow Wow Wow. Vocalist Annabella Lu-Win is a 14-year old Burmese girl Malcolm claims to have discovered in a Kilburn launderette. The backing trio has been pinched from Adam Ant, after Malcolm has failed to persuade Adam to sing the lyrics.

Malcolm has made many enemies and most record companies are very wary. He makes a deal with, of all people, E.M.I. Lightning has struck twice in the same place and soon a fantastic video is seen on Tiswas featuring Bow Wow Wow waving portable cassette-radios and sporting marvellous romantic/ethnic clothes courtesy of Vivienne Westwood. In this age of roller skates, Bow Wow Wow are the personification of Superpop.

Surprisingly the single vanishes without trace and the pantomime begins again with Malcolm claiming that it was a classic single and E.M.I. have buried the record under pressure from industry watchdogs, the B.P.I.

Soon the band are in the news again with a unique 8-song cassette which is bright yellow and has the track details printed onto the plastic and which comes in a flip-top cardboard box like a cigarette packet. The music is available only on this cassette. It is soft, pocketable, colourful and cheap and it's called *Your Cassette Pet*. You get 8 songs for £1.99, the price of a 12" disco single.

As usual, Malcolm has collaged some interesting elements: Continental soft porn, Kings Road fashion flash and the Burundi tribal beat. After Fry's Turkish Delight, we have Malcolm's Burmese delight. Pop has finally become confectionery. This small gaudy package is buttercup and bright purple and, for at least ten days, it is the future of rock & roll.

Side One kicks off with a good song, *Louis Quatorze*. "When he comes bursting through that door/My heart leaps and hits the floor/Calling himself Louis Quatorze/He's so young and dangerous." It is well-constructed, with a fast tribal drum beat, a breathy first verse, then a guitar coming in for "I love it when he says so seriously/With a gun in my back/Honey close your eyes and think of England!..."

Bow Wow Wow is the excited chatter of a teenage tease. "I feel sexy up so high/Feel my treasure chest/Lets have sex before I die/Be my special guest," she sings on *Sexy Eiffel Towers*. "I'm coming, I'm coming/I love you Eiffel Towers/You've got something I admire/I love you Eiffel Tower/Falling legs around your spire..."

The group is the subject of some debate. Either it is no mean achievement to make sex controversial in 1980 or it is an extremely mean achievement to exploit a 14-year old puppet by making her sing songs celebrating underage sex. In interviews Annabella says she is too young to be a sex object and wants to be an air-stewardess when she grows up.

Continuing his strategy of avoiding the regular rock circuit, never supporting other groups and always trying to create a new scene, Malcolm installs the band in a residency at The Starlight Roller Disco in Shepherd's Bush. The Starlight is not only the first gig Annabella has ever played, it is the first gig she has ever been to. She has never seen a group except on TV. When it comes time for the big London date they play The Rainbow at the end of February. The foyer is transformed by a candyfloss stall and Asteroid and Space Invader machines and the hall itself now has four fairground stalls where you can throw darts (three for 30p) and win Jermaine Jackson and Sheena Easton posters, and singles, and albums by acts you have never heard of.

It is the trendiest audience I have ever seen at a rock show. The ultimate in post-punk chic : lots of spiky pink hair with black stripes, plenty of pirates, earrings and headscarves, and a few purple eyebrows.

Bow Wow Wow come on at ten but without Annabella who is spotlit at the top of the helter-skelter singing *Sexy Eiffel Towers* and she continues to sing on a radio mike as she spirals down. What fun and games! What panache! Showmanship is the art of surprise. She is joined onstage by two barefoot, barelegged young dancers and the three flamboyantly gymnastic pirate girls zip through some slick dance routines. they are very colourful and glamorous. Bow Wow Wow are young, vivacious and exciting. While 400 fans bop furiously at the front, another 2000 just gawp. Maybe the trendiest pop fans are too self-conscious to let it all hang out.

The bottom line, unfortunately, is that the clothes and the performance are better than the music, which is monotonous. Bow Wow Wow are vibrant fun for ten minutes and then tedious.

THIS COULD BE YOUR LAST COSTELLO

It is Monday 29th September 1980 and I am waiting outside The Rainbow for my partner Danny, and Kevin, a young bass player from a group we used to manage, The Favourites. I start talking to a bloke and his girlfriend, and I ask them if they have seen Elvis Costello before and they say they haven't and the girl asks me if I have seen him and I reply "Yes, he's rubbish. Good records but atrocious live" and she says "Well, why are you here then?" and I say "That's a very good question."

The support band, Stray Cats, are dynamite. It is Costello's first gig in London this year. He comes on and does a new song *Shot With His Own Gun* with just voice and piano and it's not bad but during the second song I already want to leave.

The scene on the balcony is amazing, for a concert by a major act. No-one is paying any attention to the stage. People are talking, walking in and out, leaving in pairs.

Its thrasherama time, just like The Dominion. But worse. The concert is painful, crass, insulting. The group must be out of their brains. they can't *want* to sound like this. On *Less Than Zero* the drummer plays far too much and Kevin says "It's better when he tries to keep the beat, but he can't even do that!"

When they do *Chelsea* Kevin can't believe it. "It's so fast!" he gasps. *Green Shirt* is taut, tense, explosive, with some nice moody Yamaha piano, but I'm very bored. The concert seems to be taking a long time. I've been to cricket matches which were shorter. They do *Radio, Radio* which is vibrant for the first verse and then a thrash and Kevin leans over and yells "It's like the fuckin' Damned!" They're playing for themselves.

The next day I can hardly believe how bad the concert was. The source of the problem is a simple one, I think. Elvis Costello is simply not a good musician. He admits that he used to try and play with his Dad and could never get in tune. He is one of the worst guitarists I have ever heard, really a schoolboy amateur when it comes to axemanship. Knowing that he is not an ace musician himself, he should surely take pains to surround himself with good solid players.

Wild horses would not drag me to see The Attractions again, any more than they would drag me to see Blondie again. It will take me five years to forget how wretchedly self-indulgent they were, and yet Elvis Costello and the Attractions seems to be a permanent fourpiece group.

Emotionally, Elvis has a commitment to the punk revolution but his punky soul band has long outlived its usefulness. He should use loads of different bands, like David Bowie or Bob Dylan, but he doesn't seem to want to do it that way.

A few weeks later we go to see The Specials at Hammersmith Palais and I ask promoter John Curd what he thinks of Stray Cats and he says "I think they're a hype, I heard they were useless at The Rainbow." and I say "No you heard wrong. They were dynamite. Costello was awful, he wants to be The Clash" and Curdy replies "He wants to be The Clash, but he doesn't want people to know he wants to be The Clash."

STRAY CATS ROCK MARQUEE!

Outside the Marquee there is a giant Edwin Shirley truck. a rock festival artic which is half the length of Wardour Street. Who do they think they are kidding? A group playing sledgehammer skiffle on three instruments have no equipment. Their entire backline plus snare, cymbals, guitar and string bass would fit in a Honda Civic. What a hype! Pure old-fashioned rock & roll bullshit.

In the shadow of this enormous vehicle a score of surly fans stand around, ticketless and forlorn, hands in pockets, each trying to look more luckless than the next. The two shows (tonight and Monday) were instant sell-outs. Stray Cats are so hot at the moment in 1980 that the kids would not be surprised to see them burst into flames onstage.

Marquee manager Uli stands in the box office holding a fistful of green.

"Did you approach the group or did they ask to play here?" I ask.

"A bit of both," he says. "They came to me in the end."

The bar area is all Teddy boy jackets and black leather and hair which is greased up and back. At nine, Brian Setzer swans into the spotlight under a stupendous quiff, a magnificent mass of hair whose architecture is truly preposterous. A magnificent quiff. A megaquiff. He looks wild and young and mean and ready to do some rock & roll.

Stray Cats blast through three fast numbers with devastating panache and then go into a medium-tempo song which sounds like a lullaby by comparison, then a big ballad sung surprisingly well by the bass player. Then they do *Storm The Embassy*. The audience reaction, excellent so far is subdued after this song. People are not convinced that these rockabilly rebels know what they are talking about. They don't expect Lord Carrington or Henry Kissinger to get onstage with a guitar and pink socks, and they reckon these boys should be singing about girls, and blue suede shoes, not Iran.

You Can't Hurry Love is messy instrumentally, but good vocally. They should feature Brian's voice more. I remember thinking at the Rainbow that he could sing anything. I could imagine him singing *Only The Lonely* and being as commanding as Roy Orbison. In all the furore caused by his showmanship it has hardly been noticed that Brian Setzer is a great rock singer, and there is always room for another great rock singer.

For the first encore Brian is shirtless and there is a stage invasion of about 30 Teddy boys and Teddy girls, punks and skinheads. They play *Runaway Boys* again, apologising for having no more songs, Somehow, in the melée they finish it and leave the stage and the disco starts. After a minute, the lads return, all shirtless, the disco stops and they rock through another encore this time with about 60 fans onstage and five aides and bodyguards in promo T-shirts trying to keep the kids off the mikes and instruments. It is chaotic fun, and, to his everlasting credit, Brian manages to shoulder his way to the mike amid a crush of laughing, dancing bodies and scarcely misses a syllable of *Somethin' Else*. Eddie Cochrane would have been proud of him. Stray Cats are dynamite. They get a big ballsy sound from three instruments and the dynamism of their music is enhanced by the dynamism of their preformance. Brian Setzer is electrifying. He does not just make music, he makes music *happen*. Only one band in a thousand can devastate audiences the way Stray Cats have devastated The Marquee tonight. They have banished my lethargy with a bolt of lightning. It is envigorating. On the way home I sprint up the Green Park escalator steps two at a time, which I haven't done for five years.

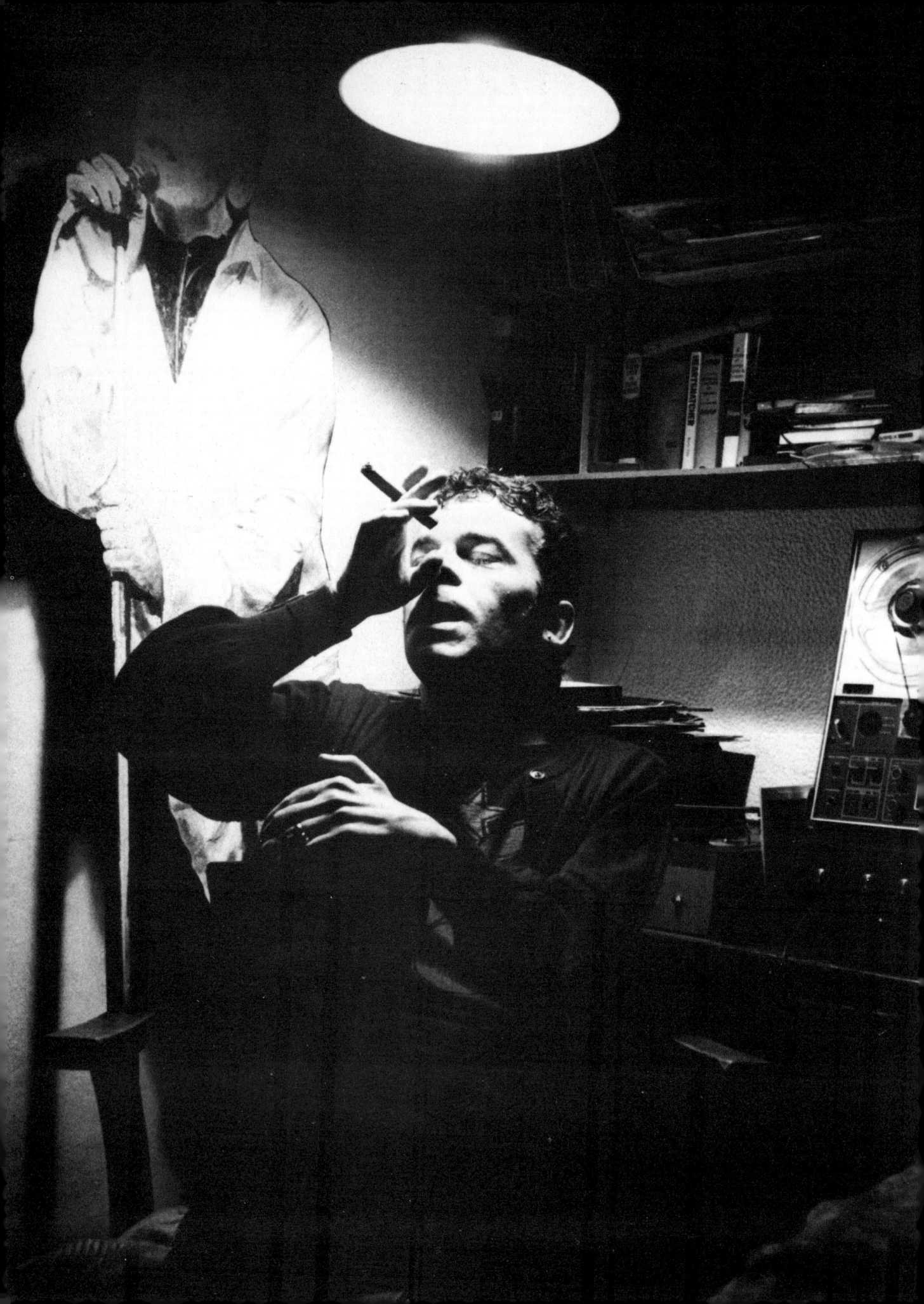

IAN DURYS
FUNK ORCHESTRA FUNK ORCHESTRA FUNK ORCHESTRA FUNK ORCHESTRA FUNK ORCHESTRA FUNK ORCHESTRA FUNK OR
ON XMAS TV

Ian Dury and the Blockheads play a concert at The Dominion on Xmas Eve 1980 which is nationally broadcast live on BBC2 television and Radio One.

The music is so earthy, playful and riotous that they make Rod Stewart sound like Barry Manilow. It is just what the doctor ordered after the disappointment of *Laughter* their third album on Stiff, which was dull fare from a man who had achieved such excellence before the departure of Chas Jankel.

At The Dominion the band is magnificent. The version of *Supermans Big Sister* is livelier and raunchier than the studio track. Guest star Don Cherry's pocket trumpet has a brilliantly ripe, ripping sound on *Yes And No (Paula)* Davey Payne's flute flutters jazzily through *Manic Depression* and the Charles/Watt-Roy rhythm section give *What A Waste* a huge, trucking sound. *Uncoolahol* is disgustingly dirty, obscene.

They play a slick instrumental chorus of *Sex and Drugs and Rock & Roll* and cruise into a smooth jazzfusion fragment of *Reasons To Be Cheerful* and then into a thunderously solid version of *Hit Me With Your Rhythm Stick.* Yes, it's nice to be a lunatic and Davey Payne's double sax rave-up is the highlight of a manic climax. The song becomes a jungle boogie, a rolling thunder revue, a transcontinental juggernaut.

No other band has their range, and no other front man has such rogueishly amusing, thoughtful and pointed spiel. His songs are so colloquial that you can't tell the words between the songs from the words of the songs, which is how it should be. Ian Dury is the finest talk-singer on the planet and the only man in history who would even consider calling an album *The Royal Academy of JacktheIademy.*

It is a winning combination of adult musicians. Ian's poetic patter is backed by music which is magnificently muscular and delicately textured. The Blockheads are an adventurous ensemble which can cruise, tease, steamroller and explode. While Ian has fun with words, they have fun with sounds. They can play rough or smooth, sounding Stonesy one moment and Crusadersy the next.

One wonders what must go through Dury's mind after such an extravaganza. Is this a dream come true? Would anyone ever dare to dream that one day a 38-year old beatnik painter would slap three kilos of grease on his hair so that he looked Gene Vincent, put on a white Teddy boy jacket with a black velvet collar and black leather gloves, and with his idol Don Cherry guesting on trumpet, star in a mature rock & roll orchestra, broadcasting live on radio and TV to an entire nation?

This show should be repeated every Xmas, and Ian Dury should be knighted and buried in Westminister Abbey. When he dies.

FUNK 77

TRUST SPRINGSTEEN

It happened that I got *Trust* the same day as I got *The River*, so this chapter was inevitable.

Elvis Costello and Bruce Springsteen are both famous rock songwriters who play guitar, and tour and record with their permanent bands. Both have released five albums. *The River* is a double LP of 20 songs and *Trust* is a single album of 14 songs. Bruce prints his lyrics, although we can hear them all. Elvis often sings indecipherably, but does not print his lyrics, because he wants to keep us guessing.

On *The River*, the material is showcased, while on *Trust*, the Attractions are showcased, and they play as if they know the material is inferior. The production of *The River* is immaculate while the production of *Trust* is crummy. Bruce's songs are carefully coloured and embellished by The E Street Band, but the Attractions just thrash their way through some remnants from the Elvis Costello songbook. It is no coincidence that the playing is better on the better songs.

The rhythms of the album are often rhythms which sound like more fun to play than they are to listen to. The sequencing is lousy. *Shot With His Own Gun* should have opened the album. The band are bored and this is the New Wave equivalent of Rod Stewart's feeble *Smiler*, the last gasp from Morgan Studios before he went to USA and used Tom Dowd and good musicians. Costello should do the same.

Bruce has been consciously diluting himself since *Born To Run*. To keep a six-piece band on the road, you have to sell records. There was nothing on his *Darkness At The Edge Of Town* album which was as eventful, exciting and expressive as the songs on his first two albums, He became safer, more pop. The music was much less street, and much less jazzy. As he challenged the audience less, he sold more records. The impressionistic rush of imagery which made his debut so thrilling was replaced by songs which were less wordy, less excessive. Bruce's music lost a lot in spontaneity and tension, although it gained a punchier sound. *Greetings From Asbury Park* and *The Wild, The Innocent And The E Street Shuffle* had more personality than any American rock albums of the mid-Seventies.

What happened was much the same as what happens when any rocker joins a corporation. After two albums, he gets taken over by the marketing department. Bruce Springsteen became popular because he allowed himself to be packaged. He wrote the same songs over and over again. He became the John O'Hara of rock & roll, a novelist of manners with an electric guitar, always escaping from the factory, driving down the dusty road, singing anthems of restlessness, chasing through the night, looking for the one face that ain't looking through him, eating his hungry heart out for some Sandy or Sherry or Candy. The playing of the E Street Band is very professional and always sympathetic to the limitations of the vocalist and to the meaning of his lyrics. Since *Born To Run* Bruce has been writing for the studio, while Elvis has just been writing for the band, and since he is a great writer but a bad musician he does a lot of rough gigs and the band develops a lot of bad habits and then goes into the studio where Nick Lowe records them as they are, rather than as they should be.

While the American's writing is linear, lateral and one dimensional, Costello is sardonic, impressionistic and ambiguous. Like Dylan, he has the gift of being meaningfully meaningless. Bruce is too earnest to have fun with language. Both are about 32, but in his heart Bruce is still 17, which is why his songs are so banal, sentimental and juvenile compared to Costello's.

The idea of doing a soul album like *Get Happy* was a good one, but the idea of doing a soul album with The Attractions was lunacy. Still, some of the material is so strong that even they can't annihilate it. Even when it's corny, Costello's wordplay is irresistible: "You lack lust, you're so lacklustre" and "Do I step on the brake to get out of your clutches /Do I speak double Dutch to a real double duchess?"

By comparison the arrangements on *Trust* are absurdly under-developed. The music and the sound are nowhere near as good as the lyrics. Most of the time The Attractions sound as if they are trying to play while falling downstairs. Musically, *You'll Never Be A Man* sounds like bad pub-rock and so does *Clubland*. *From A Whisper To A Scream* is redundant Squeezeaboogie. The band is even disappointing on the country track *Different Fingers*, although they gallop entertainingly through some good verses on *Pretty Words*, and the gloriously cheap and shiny organ on *Fish 'n' Chip Paper* is among the album's incidental pleasures.

Still, when the melody and the lyrics fall into place together, Elvis Costello still sings things you will hear from no-one else. *Big Sisters Clothes* is almost as good as *New Amsterdam*: "She's got eyes like saucers Oh you think she's a dish/ She is the blue chip that belongs to the big fish" and the hook is hard to beat: "It's easier to say I love you than yours sincerely I suppose"/"All little sisters like to try on big sister's clothes." At least the album finishes well.

If only he had the sense to open with the lines "How does it feel when you've been undressed /By a man with a mind like the gutter press.".

It is one of the current tragedies of rock music that Costello should be going backwards. For a while, the team were making all the right moves. *My Aim Is True* was a promising demo. The brilliant *This Year's Model* fulfilled that promise. *Armed Forces* was superbly streamlined, but after that it all started to go wrong. *Get Happy* was 50% soul thrash, and 50% punk bash, and however enjoyable parts of it were, it was ultimately a brilliant double demo and not a good double album.

Costello is not the first songwriter to use a tune twice (*Watch Your Step* and *Secondary Modern*), nor is he the first to issue an album of his juvenilia and outtakes, as he did with *Taking Liberties*. My objection here is not so much that *Trust* sounds like an album of outtakes, but that it sounds like a rehearsal of outtakes. Elvis has been told so often that he is a great songwriter that he may now think all his songs are great.

Still, he is major talent, and as such his follies, phobias and obstinacies are more interesting than the success of someone as bland as Springsteen, even if Bruce is the one who is having the major career. Hard-working Bruce has played Wembley and every other arena and the poor guy can't stand down for falling up.

ELVIS

THE ORDINARY BLOKE SYNDROME

The public want to believe that stars are extraordinary. People need idols, and they like to imagine that their idols are men and women of wild passions, crazy ideas and extravagant lifestyles. When punk rock emerged from the streets, its heroes were very concerned with their street credibility. For a while the notion of a "punk star" was a contradiction in terms. Joe Strummer used to let the fans sleep on the floor of his hotel room. Paul Weller was such a regular guy that he hiked round to the NME offices to give them a preview of *All Mod Cons*, the third Jam album.

Of all the groups who sought to eliminate the barriers between audience and performer, Sham 69 were the most controversial. They provoked the most frequent and violent stage invasions. Singer Jimmy Pursey used to work in a Wimpy Bar in Hersham in Surrey. No-one's material was more prosaic than his. He catalogued the everyday life of the working class teenager: football punch-ups, pulling a girl in a pub, stealing a car for a joyride, and waking up the morning after the night before. His songs were just slogans and chants. He strove mightily to avoid seeing himself as a star. His attempt to deal with the contradictions involved in being famous and being one of the lads led, in 1978, to Sham doing 'secret' gigs in pubs to 200 people to avoid riots by the wilder skinheads who followed the band. At one point Jim became so confused and depressed that he attempted suicide.

Madness also want to be just ordinary blokes. In April 1981 we began to read about the making of the Madness film. The script covers the early days of the group from 1976 to 1979, ending before their first hit record with a scene in the Dublin Castle, a pub in Camden Town. Vocalist Suggsy was quoted in Melody Maker: "We don't want to come across as anything we aren't, and that's why we're doing it in this pub. We gave out tickets to as many of the original people as we could remember and everyone will get pissed and smash a few glasses."

Chas Smith told Sounds "We don't want to act because we want to come across as normal as possible rather than phoney. It's hard because everyone's changed a lot, mellowed out." This project, directed by stiff boss, Dave Robinson, sounds a bit Brinsley Schwarzish, another case of nervous on the road and please don't ever change and all that boring old anti-star codswallop which never got anyone anywhere. It's so parochial. Where's the glamour? Where's the fantasy? Where's the international appeal? Surely kids in Brazil or Japan are more likely to want to see movie about some zany English pop stars singing their eight hit songs and larking around, than they are to want to see some ordinary blokes forming a band and playing in a pub in Camden Town? Social realism can be taken too far. The previous generation were superyobs and brilliant louts. Eric Clapton and Keith Richards are brilliant louts. Rod Stewart and Pete Townshend are superyobs. The whole appeal of Rod Stewart is that although he is one of us he is rich and larger than life and hundreds of blondes want to ride in his Rolls Royce. It was Townshend who said that he had to kick 20 photographers offstage before he could start to play at Woodstock. We want our stars to be a bit aggressive and superior. If a kid spat on Keith Richard, Keith would kick the kid in the head. Whereas George Harrison would rush offstage to have a bath. Madness gave further evidence of having no career imagination whin they played the Crystal Palace Summer In The City outdoor concert in June 1980. Ultravox did the same show when they should have waited and done a big production at Wembley Arena with the new album. These groups are very small time. They are huge in UK. They do not need the £15,000 fee from stupid gigs like these. They need to think big.

I have given away all my Madness and Ultravox records and resolved never to think about either of them again.

BRUCE FOXTON OF THE JAM

SQUEEZE — GIVE THE DOG A BONE

Squeeze started out as a South London R & B band. Their manager Miles Copeland put them in the studio with producer Muff Winwood, and after some troubled recordings Muff told Miles that they would never make records with the existing drummer. So the lads lost a year dumping the drummer, finding Gilson Lavis, and working him in.

Just as they really began to put their set together, punk became fashionable, and not being punks they were excluded from the key London venues and thus hidden from media attention. Squeeze could write and play and sing but in the summer of 1977 you needed green hair to get a review and they were playing The Brecknock and supporting the Count Bishops at The Marquee.

The failures of Squeeze at this time put paid to the notion that a band could go out and play the circuit and build up a following. This had been an obsolete idea for several years. Squeeze played exciting rock for three years, and at the end of it had no fans, because punters are deaf. They only hear what they see, and what they read. The power of the press is huge and the situation favours groups which can assert themselves verbally and visually. Groups who are not the darling of the press need to have a hit abroad first, like Dire Straits and The Police. So after an off-the-wall debut produced by John Cale (an album which featured the playing as much as the material) Squeeze went pop with *Cool For Cats* and had two big hit singles. Their third album *Argy Bargy* was *Cats* chapter two.

Argy Bargy is a particularly annoying album. It's not so much that some of it is good and some is bad. The problem is more extreme than that: half of the album is great, and the rest is terrible. Tillbrook's voice is a pop voice, not a rock voice, and his tunes are among the best in Britain. When they get a good feel on a footttapper like *Another Nail In My Heart* his voice is so light that they have to build round it carefully. His unusual guitar solo is thus spoiled by a flimsy sound. One wonders how they work. It sounds as if they write the words first, and develop clever tunes to carry the song-story. And this allows Ifford to be ridiculously wordy. People cannot remember these novellas, there are just too many lines. Squeeze's music is not accesible enough and too lyric-oriented

Squeeze should have started to make album music, the kind of music which is subtle, not bombastic. They still tend to try to play a lot of flashy tom-tom licks and flashy guitar solos which were exciting at The Brecknock, but which do not work on an album. Maybe they should get Jeff Lynne in to make them sound more like The Beatles. Maybe they should get Gilson to listen to Mike Fleetwood. Maybe they should tell Jools Holland that *Wrong Side of the Moon* is conclusive proof that vocally he is no Fats Domino. One wondered whether their fourth album would still be a load of squalid song-stories about girls who do a topless down the Surrey Docks and masturbation and VD and taking her for a spin in your stereo Jag. Could they really be so morbidly preoccupied with all this South London kitchen sink realism that they would do album after album of it?

Sure, Difford-Tillbrook music was funny and well-crafted but it was never going to sell albums abroad.

The question was: Are they just a terminally hopeless bunch of boozers, who had left their brains in a van somewhere behind a service station on the M6?

Elvis Costello raved about *Argy Bargy!* He loved it! He became Squeeze's biggest fan and championed them on Round Table, the Radio 1 review programme. So Squeeze left their manager Miles Copeland for Jake Riviera's stable! Elvis supported them at their "farewell Jools" gigs at The Albany in Deptford! Then they went to USA with him! Jake bawled out mega-mogul Jerry Moss for half an hour in the dressing room! Glen and Elvis went to Las Vagas together! Glen sang on *Trust!* But soon Jake was no longer managing Squeeze! But they were still with A & M! In fact they re-signed to do another 7 albums! They sit in a pub with NME's Nick Kent and moan about not being appreciated! They are waiting to be discovered!

Have they never seen a photo of Adam Ant? or Brian Setzer? In 7 years time they'll still be sitting in a pub waiting to be discovered after 11 albums on A & M! Squeeze are not vague enough! *Vienna* has ten lines and sold a million for Ultravox! Squeeze's songs are too parochial, too specific and too long-winded! You gotta be vaguely banal! Look at Phil Collins! Something in the air tonight, oh Lord! It's not long winded and it can mean many things to many people! It is a brilliant cliché! Like Roxy Music! Dance away your heartache, dance away! In pop you can choose your destiny! You can decide to have style! Bryan Ferry is no more handsome than Glen Tilbrook! Ferry is a working class Geordie! His Dad was a coalminer! But now he lives in a Tudor mansion in Sussex! He needs a cricket bat to fight off all the beautiful debs! That lovely young model Lucy Helmore is going to marry him! He's 35, She's 19!!!
But wait! What about *East Side Story*, this new Squeeze album produced by Elvis Costello and his engineer Roger Bechirian! Elvis is bold! Adventurous! Never goes further than far too far! Not scared to take chances! And here he tries a lot of studio tricks! They do a five-minute maudlin country song! And the last song is a throwaway rockabilly tune! But they only let new man Paul Carrack sing one song! One lousy song out of 14! What a mean load of bastards! Paul has a great soul voice! But Difford hasn't written a great soul lyric, just his usual wordy story! How long has this been going on? Five years!
Some of the rhythms really plod! Plod, Plod, Plod! And they're not as clever as 10CC! *Rubber Bullets* was topical! And 10CC did not live south of the river. The writing's been on the wall for years! I just couldn't see it! Squeeze's indie EP was called *Packet Of Three!* In the age of the pill, they are into condoms! They are losers! They are living in another century down there! One song *Quintessence* is produced by Dave Edmunds and it sounds

TILLBROOK AND DIFFORD

like the Attractions! Squeeze get happy! Costello has got Gilson playing less and on one track not playing at all! This is progress! He has shown them maybe 70% of a new direction! Will the bozos of Deptford ever find true happiness? Nick Lowe is doing their fifth album! Who will produce them after that? Who can do something with England's most boring, talented group?

This exclamatory style has been nicked from American writer Lester Bangs! He wrote me a mad letter once! After I'd written a mad letter to him! Hello, Lester!

Spandau and the New Romantic Blitz

Rock club and pubs are pleb, but discos are smart. Originally, the New Romantic audience used to frequent Chaguaramas, a gay disco which closed and re-opened as The Roxy in 1976. The punk explosion pushed everything else into the background for many months.

Punk was social realism, but romantic escapism needed its own showcase. In late 1977 Rich Kids drummer Rusty Egan and Steve Strange began to hire a drinking club called Billy's every Friday and run "Bowie nights" for style-conscious teenagers. Rusty was the DJ and he played Roxy Music and Kraftwerk as well as David Bowie records and black soul.

The Rich Kids were falling apart but had some studio time in which Midge Ure and Rusty cut some demos with as Visage with Steve singing. Ultravox's Billy Currie was also involved in early Visage recordings. They played the tapes on the disco at Billy's but did not get a record deal at first. Steve later ran another club called Blitz.

Two participants in the club scene were brothers Gary and Martin Kemp, a couple of working class teenagers from Islington who were on the dole but managed to go out a lot and liked style. They hated slumming it in cheap boozers full of pleb youths, and formed a group to cater to the underground élite of fancy-dressed kids. To make it even more élite, they only played once a month, and the cult heard about the gigs by word-of-mouth.

Was Spandau Ballet as simple as that? Not quite. Although it is popularly assumed that Spandau dropped out of the sky wearing kilts and table cloths round their shoulders, they used to be a powerpop group called The Makers who played scruffy pubs like The Brecknock and The Hope before it dawned on them that the pub-rock circuit is a loser scene where punters ask themselves the inevitable question: "If this group is any good, what are they doing playing in a dump like this?"

Realising that working class kids want to get away from poverty and not celebrate it by wearing punk rags, they were able to re-invent themselves. Their tactics were innovative, even if their music was not.

Journeys To Glory is a flimsy first album by a shallow young group who were so flushed by their success in securing a big deal and their own Reformation label that they rushed straight into the studio with producer Richard James Burgess, a drummer with a poncey jazzrock group called Landscape. To release any first album before Xmas would have been marketing suicide, so they had a hit with their only decent song *To Cut A Long Story Short* and buried the album until March. They should have buried it permanently, since it is one of the most mannered, heartless, witless, poorly-played and tedious records ever made.

Still, Spandau have a lot of career imagination to make up for their lack of musical imagination. While Squeeze were sitting in a boozer in Deptford discussing their just-released fourth album, Spandau Ballet were in New York opening The Underground, a chic new disco, with a combined gig, fashion show and press party. They had taken over some of their friends and designers. These were smarter tactics than those employed by Roxy Music who kicked off in basketball stadiums supporting Jethro Tull and died the death of all deaths. One wondered whether Spandau had in fact discovered their true métier. Should they now fly round the world, opening every new disco in every country, forever? Or would it pall after a while since the discos would always be new, but Spandau would soon become just another group from last year? Many people found the bumptiousness of Spandau a bit hard to swallow. They were novices whose every interview contained pompous boasts like "There's no-one over 23 involved" and "There was no group we wanted to go and see." Spandau were the logical conclusion of 30 years of amplified music. It had to happen. It had taken a long time but now in 1981 it was a reality: Spandau Ballet, the group for people who don't like groups. It was enough to make you vomit all over their tasteful white-on-white album cover.

UB40S

RUBBER BALCONY RUBBER BALCONY RUBBER BALCONY RUBBER BALCONY RUBBER BALCONY

A good group should be able to make an album which lasts their fans until their next album comes out. For an album to last nine months or more it needs to be packed with good songs and good playing, and the only group to produced two quality albums in succession is the Beat.

Wha'ppen? is the album of 1981. There is not one duff track on it. The Beat simply have more good tunes and more to say than any other group around at the moment. The album is less obvious, more textured than it's predecessor *I Just Can't Stop It*, which had a clean mix, strong, simple top lines, and a marvellous headlong vitality.

The Beat write together and credit all the songs to The Beat and their arrangements sound organic, as if each number has been thoroughly kicked around in rehearsal so that it becomes a maximum workout for everybody. *Wha'ppen?* has a wonderful mixture of melody and muscularity, roughness and smoothness, accessibility and adventurousness. It is easy-going but socially aware, listenable but relevant, and so well-crafted that it makes *Zenyatta Mondatta* sound like a demo. The music rolls and throbs along, but it also challenges. It is much more of a reggae album than the first one, although The Beat are basically a songs band who are beginning to get into reggae playing, unlike UB40 who were always a reggae band. Still, it remains very much The Beat; *Get A Job*, with that burning, buzzing, bouncing bass riff could not be any other group.

When I first heard *Don't Slow Down* on the radio I knew it was UB40, even though their sound had changed dramatically. They were much more solid on the bottom, and much more rich and succulent on top. *Signing Off* had superfeel, but *Present Arms* has supersound. June release was just right. UB40 are sunshine on a cloudy day, perfect music for a rainy English summer.

The songwriting on *Present Arms* is patchy. When the album is good, it is very good. *One In Ten* is a great idea for a song: "I am the one in ten a number on a list/I am the one in ten even though I don't exist/Nobody knows me though I'm always there/A statistical reminder of a world that doesn't care." The song starts with the chorus and they give it a solid dance groove. "My arms enfold the dole queue, malnutrition dulls my hair/My eyes are black and lifeless with an underprivileged stare/I'm the beggar on the corner will no-one spare a dime/I'm the child that never learns to read because no one spares the time." It's a great song, powerfully uptempo and magnificently uncompromising: "I'm a middle-aged businessman with chronic heart disease/I'm another teenage suicide on a street that has no trees."

Don't Slow Down is a pure pop song, sweet and persuasive, with lusciously lazy horns. *Sardonicus* is one of the best songs they have written and a reminder that their best tracks are often the ones where the music most suits the husky vocal style of lead singer Al Campbell. The feel of *Silent Witness* is wondrously spititual. The rest of the album is filler. Some of it good filler, admittedly.

In other words, *Present Arms* is a typical second album. The group, having used most of their best songs, is trying hard to make a technically superior record and has inevitably lost some of the unique flavour, which made them so appealing in the first place. UB40's debut was a hard album to follow. *Signing Off* is the best feel album ever recorded by a British group, and the only independent LP ever to make No 1. It sold over 350,000 in the UK alone, an astonishing total these days.

The Beat and UB40 are two of Britain's most important groups. Both are playing ethnic pop deluxe, but at the moment UB40 are only scoring four out of ten for songwriting where The Beat are scoring eight or nine. In time, I expect that UB40 will write, play and sing an album which has both superfeel and supersound.

On June 22nd, 1981 I saw UB40 play the National Club in Kilburn, a large Irish ballroom which on this occasion held a bigger crowd than ever before, close to 4000. The evening was a revelation. I had expected music which was mellow, moody and atmospheric. I thought they were a slightly anonymous underground pop-reggae band and was shocked (and thrilled) to see a wild dance party with thousands of kids bopping like mad and singing along on every song. The energy-level of the audience was unreal. I was not ready for UB40-mania.

All eight members of the band wore T-shirts, and there was a lot of red light on the stage. They are selling warmth, and they know it. UB40 turned concrete into rubber: the balcony was bouncing up and down at least an inch, and it made one realise that they should only play in places which are structurally secure and have very solid foundations.

The · Finest · Group · In · Britain

The Belle Stars have the prettiest guitarist I have ever seen. She has fabulously feathered headgear like a classy French stripper, and the other six girls are an avalanche of multi-coloured mini-dresses and fruity sombreros as they stroll onto the stage of the Hammersmith Palais in June 1981.

Five of them used to be in another group called The Bodysnatchers who were fun for ten minutes on 2-Tone. When I saw them at Dingwalls they did not have many decent songs, but they had a distinctively friendly, girlish sound, and they moved well.

Now the music is crass, charmless and dull, a burpy blitzkreig. I cannot understand why they should want to sound so loud and ballsy. I never dreamed that The Belle Stars would actually be *worse* than The Bodysnatchers.

A spooky electronic reggae tape plays and Ranking Roger romps into the centre of the stage and the lead guitarist, his hair rocker-style, lunges forward to the crowd crushed at the front and gives someone his drink in a paper cup and The Beat motor into *Too Nice To Talk To*.

And how they motor!

The sound of the Beat is awesome and overwhelming. They are amazingly solid and sparse. Their ensemble sound has a dimension of muscular authority, which is entirely lacking in Madness or The Specials. The difference is astounding. The Beat have so much more range and control and power, there is no comparison. They are in another league altogether. What the others are attempting, The Beat are actually delivering. Needless to say it is trampoline time on the dance floor, thousands of heads bobbing up and down like mad. The twin-vocal attack is wonderful. The Beat's clothes are as street as can be. Roger is in tracksuit trousers, red sweatshirt and familiar black hat. The rest of the band are in T-shirts, except Dave Wakeling who wears a classy light brown short-sleeved shirt, a tiny concession to their pop star status.

Get A Job is colossal, with Saxa punctuating the rhythm rush with huge blaring, stabbing slabs of sound. This is it. Fun with an edge. What a monster song! "There's a training course where boys and girls of real ambition start a new job in a factory where they're making ammunition ..."

As the dance action slows for *Psychedelic Rockers* scores of fans filter off the floor towards the bar, and I drift upstairs, where bodies are packed four deep on the balcony and fans too small to see are skanking sweatily and merrily.

The concert ends after 50 minutes. The set has been tightly packed with powerfully played uptempo songs. With so many good bass riffs, The Beat can sustain the propulsion of their set beyond anything I have seen for years, and the commitment they inspire in their audience is phenomenal. They play powerfully. They mean it. Drummer Everett Morton means it because before The Beat he worked for 12 years in a factory. For *Tears Of A Clown* hundreds of hands reach up and clap along very fast, as if on some pre-arranged signal. More hands go up for *Stand Down Margaret* and the boys stop playing to let the crowd sing along. People in the *bar* are dancing to *Twist And Crawl*.

Clearly, they are a relevant dance band. Any group could be hip and use reggae poet Linton Kwesi Johnson as compere, but not every group has an audience who knows who Linton is and would cheer him before and after he does a poem just prior to the appearance of the headliners. The Beat are pop and street in a way that, perhaps, only The Who have been in the past, and they may become as crucial to the Eighties as The Who were to the Sixties. Certainly the audience base is there. They can draw 3000 plus in every major city in Britain and they can leave them high and satisfied. Their audience is under-23 and it wears jeans and it is building solidly. It is not a fashion crowd which will hop onto some other trendy group next year. I have the feeling that these kids are ready and willing to buy Beat records for the rest of the Eighties, if those records are of the same high quality as they have been so far.

There is no better group in Britain. The Blockheads at the Roundhouse played as powerfully, but Dury was annoyingly actorish, forever posing with props and handkerchiefs, and I walked out before the end. At he moment The Beat are almost too uncompromising for their own good. Their marketing could be a little bit more mainstream, and they seem to be aware of the dilemma; the front cover of *Wha'ppen* is too ethnic, and the back cover is too pop. They could afford to dress up just a little bit more next year. If any group has earned the right to be a shade more flash, they have.

There are dozens of hairy, denim-jacketed youths around in Hammersmith tube station, so I figure there must have been a heavy metal concert at The Odeon tonight. On the train a youth with long hair, flared jeans and a rolled-up poster in his hand comes in and sits across from me.

"Who was on tonight? I ask.
"Ted Nugent."
"Was he loud?"
"Yes!"
"How long did he play for?"
"Two hours."
"Does he have a trio, or what?"
"He had four guitarists . . ."
"Jesus Christ!"
"He got rid of his bass player and drummer from last year and now he's got three other guitarists besides himself."
"Bloody hell!"
"He was great!"
The kid looks whacked and admits he has been overdiong it.
"I saw Whitesnake at the weekend and Status Quo last week."
"Have you seen Def Leppard?"
"Yeah, saw them supporting AC/DC."
"Ever seen Zeppelin?"
"No, my brother saw them at Knebworth last year."
"Year before."
"Right."
"I saw them at the Lyceum before you were born. It was the first time a group had charged £1 for a show. Just before the second album came out."

UK and USA

Just then a girl sits down directly opposite me. Short honey blonde hair, smart new black jeans, primrose T-shirt with small Beat badge. She is 15 and lovely, too nice to talk to to.
"Have you seen The Beat before?" I ask.
"No."
"Magic aren't they?"
"Yes!"
We chat about the show and she gets off at Paddington, having admitted that the last group she saw was The Members at the Nashville, which I realise must have been over a year ago. The Nashville was closed after a series of busts for underage drinking. It seems that the appeal of The Beat is so powerful that they are selling tickets to girls who don't go to concerts. That is success. Kids who never go to gigs are going to see The Beat!
Oddly enough, Dave Wakeling is standing right next to us the next night at the Lyceum for the Prince gig. It is soon obvious that Prince is no singer, and no guitarist. When I remark that he sounds as if he hasn't played the guitar for three weeks, Danny says "He got someone else to do the soundcheck for him!" After a fast-moving hour of power from The Beat last night, 50 minutes of fake funk from Prince seems to last a month. In his worst moments he comes over like the Sammy Davis Jr. of disco. He is a fair performer with some flashey moves and a few good ideas, but he desperately needs a co-writer, a producer and a decent band. At the moment he is just a bit of fun, a naughty little Muppet who sings "I'll take you to the movies, we'll sit in the back, I'll jack you off, I'll jack you off..."
For the second encore *Uptown* he climbs up again on the P.A. cabinet and poses and plays ferociously but when he jumps off, I notice that his guitar is not even plugged in. That sums up the evening. Modern masturbation toys, no electricity.
Earlier on I resisted the temptation to lean over and tell Dave Wakeling that I had seen The Beat last night and that they were 500 times better than Prince. I'm sure he knew, anyway.

✗✗✗✗✗✗ SEX ✗✗✗✗✗✗✗✗
is here to stay

Sexual charisma.
Jimi Hendrix had it. Mick Jagger and Michael Jackson have it. Diana Ross has it. John Travolta has it.
Unfortunately, New Wave has very little of it. Paul Weller looks like a wages clerk. Joe Strummer looks like a bus conductor. The Undertones look like urchin schoolboys. XTC look like bourgeois schoolboys. Rockpile look like schoolboys parents. Although astonishingly pretty in real life, Toyah always looks like a wrestler on TV.
In the sex sweepstakes, almost everyone is a non-starter. When a good-looking newcomer like Kim Wilde appears, and for her second single has a video which includes scenes with her being photographed in the shower by a cheeky band member, and vamping naughtily, she makes a big impact. There is always room for a pretty blonde with a good voice.
Generally, New Wave has a lot going for it. The musical talent is there. The commitment is there. There are good singers and good players and loads of groups with interesting image ideas, but there is a real lack of sex appeal.
The only three personalities who make it on that level are Debbie Harry, Sting and Adam Ant. Sting is king, Debbie is the princess of pop, and Adam is the dashing prince.
Debbie Harry's image has taken Blondie a long way. When they first played the Rainbow they played too fast. too loud and too long. They were a typical American band: no confidence. They confused speed with energy and Debbie's "dancing" consisted of wiggling about as if she was standing on broken glass.
No amount of volume can conceal the fact that Blondie's sound is as flimsy as a matchbox. The drummer is a thrasher. They have no rhythms. Their material is not rock, it is pop and they are not tight enough to play pop, even if pop worked in concert, which it doesn't.
At the time I wondered whether Debbie should be more casual and low-key and try to become Lou Reed with tits, or whether she should do a caricature of male rock star machismo, which might be amusing. Anyway, having learned their lesson, they came back and played the smaller, more intimate Roundhouse and that was a fair lightweight thrash in a party atmosphere.
Then, when they were the biggest-selling group in the UK, they returned and played a week at the Odeon, a cinema which is even bigger than The Rainbow. Debbie has improved enormously and she moved well and sang well but the band was still atrocious, sloppy beyond belief. One guitarist who could play would be much better than two who can't. I have rarely heard or seen anything as lame and absurb as Blondie encoring with a James Brown number.
Blondie completely fail to recognise their limitations. They should tighten up and play their greatest hits for 50 minutes maximum. They should just play their hits as tightly and professionaly as possible and never, never attempt to jam or solo. Debbie should dash off and do a couple of costume changes to keep the crowd awake. Then they might be slick and snappy, instead of being messy and feeble.
Inevitably, Blondie were warmly received but the fact is that by the time a group are playing to 25,000 fans in one city, they are playing to people who do not know the front end of a group from the back. Many of these punters have never seen a good group on a good night.
Of course, Debbie is not phenomenally beautiful or even particularly attractive, but she is miraculously photogenic. She also writes some good lyrics. Mostly, Blondie are a singles band

ADAM ANT

rather than an album band. *Auto America* is flimsy and inconsequential, half glossy schmalz, half bantamweight popfunk. *Rapture* is a travesty which could have been a classic single. The groove isn't even as good as the Philly groove on the David Bowie records. Although they have the wit to be the first white group with a big rap record, Debbie sings the first half of the song, and by the time she starts to rap the feel is so fake, so false, that the chance has gone. They have never sounded so lost, or more like producer's puppets.

The best track is the only one not written by the band. *The Tide Is High* is the cover girl's best cover. The lyrics are a marketing man's dream and her vocal performance has never been more warmly seductive, more friendly, more humourous. The fantasy potential of Debbie singing these words is enormous: "Every girl wants you to be her man, but I'll wait my dear till it's my turn, I'm not the kinda girl who gives up just like dat, oh no ... the tide is high I'm holding on, I'm gonna be your number one, number one, the tide is high but I'm holdin on, I'm gonna be your number one, number one."

Debbie singing this was almost as good, almost as suggestive, as Marilyn Monroe singing "I wanna be loved by you, by you, and nobody else but you."

In the BBC documentary *The Police In The Far East,* Sting looked fabulous. He was the most beautiful human I have seen since the ravishing Nadia Comaneci at Strasbourg, a gymnastics

competition a few years ago. As he sang *Message In A Bottle* in a wonderful green, black and flame cardigan, Sting looked more like a star than anyone on the planet. He was the stuff of dreams.

The film showed us everything we might have expected. Manager Miles Copeland told us that "Bombay, India's never had a rock show at all!" A smart Oriental Carly Simon lookalike got Sting's autograph and smiled vacuously. In Tokyo the audience was all teenage girls and in Bombay it was all blokes with beards and moustaches. We saw tour manager Kim Turner chatting into his walkie-talkie. We saw Andy play sitar while Sting told interviewer, Ann Nightingale that his Dad was a milkman. At times his voice was hoarse, no doubt from singing "I can't, I can't, I can't stand losing you" 700 times too often. We saw Andy and Stewart and Sting in rickshaws and on camels. As *Roxanne* played, we saw pyramids. Sting sounded good but looked incredible, like one of the titans of mass entertainment. He has some of the charm of Paul McCartney, some of the toughness of John Lennon and some of the athleticism of Rod Stewart. He is a rock conquistador, impossibly handsome, impossibly self-assured and impossibly successful. He is the personification of pop charisma and for The Police to have this film shown in a week when both album and single are No. 1 is a reminder to all other groups that this scale is what they should aspire to.

AAAANTMANIAAAAA

The ghost of Mark Bolan is crooning gently over the P.A. "You're dirty sweet and you're my girl" sighs Marc, "Bang a gong, get it on, get it on ..."
The support group Altered Images arrive on the stage of The Dominion, Tottenham Court Road.
louder, almost to the threshold of pain. Suprisingly, they shamble off after about 20 minutes with one guitarist giving us a petulant V-sign. "Same to you!" shouts a male voice behind me. Quite! Never blame the audience. What do they expect after one single? Mass adulation?
Looking around the balcony during the interval, it's all cavalier shirts with extra-baggy sleeves, pirate boots, black leather trousers and white moccasins. Two-thirds of the audience are girls between 13 and 18, chewing gum, chattering eagerly, some wearing no make-up at all, just jeans and sweaters, others with tiny ribbons in their hair, crosses on their cheeks and white warpaint stripes across their noses.
There are murmurs of expectation now. Bryan Ferry sings "It's a hard, it's a hard it's a hard rain's gonna fall." Chugalong soothing pop for ageing romantics. Some of the house lights dim, slowly. It is still only 8.50 p.m. The kids are patiently impatient: cheers, whistles and isolated screams as Bowie sings "FAAAAAAAAAAME" and the drums thud, and when an organ-sax instrumental record comes on there are jeers from a crowd whose good-humoured abuse is now edgy, nervous, almost angry ...
A chant starts: "WE WANTS THE ANTS! WE WANT THE ANTS!
And the curtain goes up to reveal eight amber spotlights behind two raised drum kits and all of a sudden it's bedlam on the balcony and I have a memory jump, a flashback to the ABC Ardwick in 1965 when I saw The Beatles.
Ex-Roxy bassist Gary Tibbs is blond and barechested. Adam sings "Dog! eat! Dog! eat! Dog!" Adam is a knee-slapping slick-punching, leather-trousered, war-painted rock & roll warrior. Fat guitarist Marco has two red skull-and-crossbones flags on his chest. As the band plays the intro to the fourth number a girl in the row behind me recognises it and squeals "I love this!" and for *Don't Be Square Be There* Adam's guitar is brought on and it has a treblier sound than Marco's and, of course, two skull-and-crossbones stickers on it and he sings his anthem "Antmusic for sexpeople/sexmusic for Antpeople" and the next number is the best so far, a whirring, roaring, jumping noise which catapults hundreds of fans on the balcony to their feet. This song has a great feel, whatever it's called.
Then they do *Ants Invasion* and *Killer In The Home* with the two drummers working really well together. Both numbers end in darkness and wild applause. Then comes the powerfully insistent, grinding *Dirk Wears White Socks*. One drummer comes down to the front to add vocals on a number, which includes the lines, "She heard voices from Outer Space." Soon Adam is asking "Won't You Come To Paris With Me," and you know he would need ten jumbojets to accommodate all the volunteers. The other drummer descends to add a squeaky alto sax solo.
There is plenty of punky percussion and on another fast-racing number Adam twirls a swagger stick and on *Jolly Roger* he jams four fingers in his mouth and lets loose a glorious whistle: "It's your money that we want and your money we shall 'ave!" and smoke bombs explode vividly, and then it's "Unplug the jukebox and do us all a favour/That music's lost its taste so try another flavour." Ant Music. And then into "We are family, a wild nobility" and a barrage of coloured lights flashing ... Antpeople are the warriors yeaaeaheah!!!!!!!
Backlit by eight green and eight amber lights, Adam stands on a light cabinet on the left of the stage. The sound is an avalanche of tom-toms as he pulls his Hussars jacket. The balcony is shaking underfoot. The set ends after an hour of romantic escapism. The costumes are crucial. Costumes are for people playing a part, and if they are playing a part it's not real and if it's not real, it is safe. Adam and the Ants are as safe as ice-cream. Soon, amid mayhem (screaming, whistling and clapping) five figures race back onstage and do *"A.N.T.S."* to the tune of *"Y.M.C.A."* as a fun second encore and after faking collective indecision about whether to leave the stage again they do one more. Adam rips off his shirt after five minutes of teasing, and they climax by throwing the drumsticks high into the crowd. Adam and the Ants have enough ideas for a show, but not enough good songs, but they carry it on the performance. Adam is glamorous, masculine and vividly athletic, full of authoritative movements, far ahead of Bowie, almost in the Rod Stewart class as a performer. The band are good players, and the overall level of showmanship is excellent. They may play Wembley Arena in 1982 but this is their moment. *Kings Of The Wild Frontier* is the No. 1 album nationwide and has been on the charts for 19 weeks. The tabloid dailies, always more interested in phenomena than in music, are giving them huge headlines.
Today's *Sun* centrespread headline is "ANTMANIA." Reporter Nina Myskow covered the Newcastle and Glasgow Apollo dates of this mini-tour. "This week, as rock's newest sex symbol and his band of four pirates swashbuckled their way round Britain on their first tour since the group's sensational chart success, I heard a sound that has been missing from rock for many years. The sound of girls screaming their hearts out for their hero." She continued: "Wild and very sexy, he whirls and turns, struts and jumps, fur and feather flying, leather gleaming. It is a performance of superstar quality."
The *Sunday Mirror* centrespread headline is "LORD OF THE ANTS" and Adam tells Colin Wills that sex is the greatest adventure and that he turns sex into fantasy. It's all good clean fun, says Adam.

UK and USA

American groups take a professional attitude to being in a group, whereas British groups take an emotional attitude to it. The Ramones can pretend to be brothers for six years but the Sex Pistols cannot pretend to be friends for more than two. In an interview the typical American will use the word 'career' at least 58 times, but the British musician will not use the word at all.

Attitudes to the music business itself are vastly different, too. In London, record executives are often treated like parasites, whereas in New York they are invariably treated like royalty. When Clive Davis and his entourage go to a gig they have their own table or their own box, and it is like Caesar's visit to the gladiators: thumbs up, or thumbs down.

Because of the size of America, record companies are more important than groups. The business in USA tends to work in a way which encourages the formation of a super-league of faceless mega-stars. The groups which are biggest are of the Boston-Foreigner-Styx-REO Speedwagon variety, and none of them have any personality.

This means that the kids do not really care about the group. The audience do not really identify with the artists in the way that they did in the past, and if there is no loyalty, there is no build; and if there is no build, there is no career. Boston were a typical high technique/low personality act. Their first album did eight million, the second album did four million, and after that they were in trouble.

Of course, it's true that many people like music without personality. I saw Tangerine Dream at the Albert Hall in 1974 and they were peaceful in the way that a silent TV screen is peaceful: you watch a picture which is replaced by another picture, which is replaced by yet another picture. You can look away and look back and be confident of not having missed too

much. Tangerine Dream played a 70-minute set of astral lullabies, bass pulses and choral sounds, and then a 30-minute second set. It was Eurojazz for the mandrax generation. Three long-haired Germans in coloured darkness must be the ultimate in anti-personality. They did not introduce themselves or the pieces they played and they did not wave or bow or give any visual or verbal clue whatever. And, of course, with three synthesiser players, it was impossible to tell who was playing what. A kid two rows below me was peering at the stage through binoculars, and I guessed he was looking not at the performers, but at the equipment.

The Damned have taken a very British approach to their career as punks. They broke up, reformed minus one member, and then, when the heavy metal boom happened, they went heavy metal when they should have been consolidating their unique status as original punks.

With so many of the early punk bands going commercial, or electronic, the Damned had the chance to soldier on and become a performing legend. They would have been the sole survivors of the spirit of '77, playing to kids who were too young to have seen them then, but who would enjoy a good jolt of authentic pogonoise. Instead, they have been superceded by The Dead Kennedys, who have brought a touch of American perseverance and professionalism to the cause of hard punk with records like *Too Drunk To Fuck*.

Where British groups often survive on sheer flair, the Americans value craftsmanship. Their more professional approach to recording has often been evident. Recording a large British group is invariably a nightmare. It is hard to get an arrangement eight people are happy with. The Blockheads broke up six times during the recording of their second album. At one point, tempers frayed so badly that Ian Dury was actually banned from the studio. The Specials broke up five times during the recording of *More Specials* which is hardly surprising with a sevenpiece band containing a soul drummer, a soul bassist, a punk guitarist, a punk singer, two West Indians, who are into reggae and nervous composer/producer, Jerry Dammers, on organ.

Fans rarely realise how brain-damaging recording can be. As the hours go on and on and the lights dim in the room with chocolate carpet on the walls, the giant electronic desk begins to look like a city from 20,000 feet, a huge area of coloured lights, a world in itself, a metropolis of wires and pulses, a mini-empire of knobs and buttons and faders over which the engineer's fingers glide and touch in movements – sometimes stabbing, sometimes slow – while all the time the lights blink and flicker and the 24 VU meters spurt up cream columns into amber and sink to spurt up again, and all the time you're listening to the same song, or parts of the same song, again and again and again.

However luxurious, the studio is an unnatural and claustrophobic environment. After a mere six hours I start to suffer from severe sensory overload, and I go home and start behaving strangely. And I know that I am more stable and sensible than most musicians, so what does it do to them after 14 hours, or 22 hours?

No wonder they take drugs to keep going. No wonder they make mistakes. No wonder they have car crashes at dawn. No wonder people get sick of recording and want to stop, even when they are not finished, although sometimes they don't know whether they are finished.

Consider recent Talking Heads and recent Costello. *Remain In Light* is an album where the production is better than the material, and *Trust* is one where the material (although not Costello's best) is superior to the sound, the playing and the mix. *Remain* is a progression, *Trust* is a regression.

Knowing as we do the Americans fondness for high-tech, it is no surprise to find that the Talking Heads album is an album of sounds, an imaginative series of noises and voices, a sonic story meticulously unfolded, so that, at times, the production is so good that it becomes the material, as Side Two gets slower, spacier, and doomier.

Of course, the imperfections of *Trust* are just as interesting as the perfections of *Remain In Light,* and more so as the listener has time to become fully acquainted with both. A record is a record and it stays the same, but people are people, and people can get used to anything, even crummy Costello. After a while, you listen to what's there, and not to what should be there.

The B-52s are a good example of what happens to American groups. Their debut has personality. It was lively because it was produced by Chris Blackwell and British engineer Robert Ash. The jagged, toppy guitar sound on *Hot Lava* was very lively, and sounded like a group playing. *Planet Claire* with its robotic throb and spacey organ, had a lot of wit and personality. They were a very promising bunch of young college kids.

Wild Planet, their second album, is taut and textured, a perfect engineer's album. An album of sounds rather than songs. The only track on which the hook and the performances are strong enough to complete with the sounds is *Private Idaho*. While the first album is casual, rough and dynamic, the second is very manufactured. Everyone is trying so hard, it has stopped sounding like fun. One beings to wonder whether The B-52s are part of the disposable junk culture which they started out satirising. Are they now last year's entertainment craze, a one-idea band without the star or the songwriter to sustain a major career? Are they programmed to self-destruct? Will they go the same way as hula-hoops and beach movies? Will another quintet of smart, bored college kinds come along and mention The B-52s in their debut album and complete another cycle of planned obsolescence?

Back in April 1979 British radio producer John Walters wrote a good article in The Listener:

"I remember a punk fan saying to me in 1976 that the importance of the Pistols was that they challenged the established order in a way that the average kid daren't – but

would like to. They were mad enough to use themselves as guinea pigs to define what could or couldn't be done…A society in which the young unquestioningly accept the artistic, social and moral ideals of their elders is either primitive or declining."
Walters described how he had embarked somewhat cagily on his first visit to the USA, and soon figured out something which took me at least six visits: "I had always assumed that the lack of success, Stateside, for British new wave was a plot on the part of Big Business, but after only a short time, I realised something which years of playing their records and watching *Bonanza* and *Kojak* hadn't revealed to me. America is a foreign country! They do things differently and think differently. I talked to people in records and radio about what we did and they were interested, but invariably said 'But the bottom line is, does it make money?' In Britain rock is about change and challenge; in America, it is about acceptance and conformity. And making money."

John would probably agree that The Buzzcocks are a typical British band, and that Bruce Springsteen is a typical American band. One does four albums and breaks up, the other does four albums and turns into a machine for making money.
Record Mirror's Mike Gardner interviewed Linx after they had just returned from their first recordings in USA. The young British funksters were astounded by the professionalism of the Americans. Singer David Grant said "The session musician's attitude to music in L.A. is serious. It's business and if you hire a guitarist for three o'clock then at ten minutes to three his two roadies will turn up with a huge flight case that has all his guitars and another with all his effects.
"They set it all up and all he had to do is play. I'm sure if he could have arranged it he would have let them wheel him in on a bed. At the end he just put his guitar down and left and the roadies took the stuff down. He was so good that he was in and out in half an hour. This guy's only 21…it's amazing."
Several years ago I was chatting to Nick Lowe in the artists' bar at the Hammersmith Odeon and asked if he was going to produce Clover, as was rumoured, and he said he felt they were so good they should be produced by "someone who really knows the desk."
In June 1979 Lowe was interviewed at length by Nick Kent in NME and declared: "I want to make records people will like and that I can be proud of. When I say I've bumbled through, I mean, I listen to, say, a Jeff Lynne record and that sounds to me like a craftsman's record. I could never make records like that. I just haven't got the patience."
Two years later, remixed American pressings of *Trust* appeared in the import racks of London record shops. While Nick and Elvis can't be bothered to get it right, the Americans are pros and keen to shift some product. When I saw the words TRUST REMIX I just grinned, for it was explicit evidence of everything I have always said about British groups in general and Costello in particular.

NICK LOWE

EPILOGUE

So where does all this leave us?
Clearly, The Sex Pistols were a major event among young people. Malcolm McLaren was the catalyst who sparked a revolution. Chris Thomas got the killer vocal from Johnny Rotten. Chrissie Hynde is the first woman to sing rock. Ian Dury is the best disc-jockey in the world. Debbie Harry is the most photogenic songwriter in the world. The Clash are absurdly over-rated. Squeeze are an example of talent without imagination, whilst Spandau Ballet are an example of imagination without talent.
I'm glad The Police got lucky because they worked hard through years of poverty and rejection. Elvis Costello can write rings, triangles and parallellograms round anyone in USA but he can't make a decent record. The Beat and UB40 are fun with an edge. Pop is ephemeral. My favourite verse this week is from "Cheated" by The Beat: "A valentine from a politican/Three pages of your dog's ambitions/The stabbed lover and the furious bunny/You stare to long and your eyes go funny" and much as I love those words, I love them more when I can hear them with the rhythm and the sound and the melody.
The UK is a major talent source but not a major source of professionalism. American groups are in it for a career and British groups are in it for a laugh. Some groups make music, and others make music *happen*. Sex is here to stay. However big you think their egos are, they are always bigger. Musicians are the biggest groupies of all. Music keeps popping up in places where it is most appropriate and most useful.
At this point I'm reluctant to reduce everything to Palmerisms since that would be the ultimate laziness as well as the ultimate arrogance, compressing everything into one-liners when I know that everything should be examined and discussed on its own terms. It's just that I agree with Quentin Crisp's dictum about the pleasure to be derived from sweeping statements.
Overall, in New Wave, there is a shortage of good voices, and a shortage of musicians who can write a good album. There are too many minor talents and too many ifs. The previous generation was simpler to understand. The Beatles were megastars. Mick Jagger and Jimi Hendrix had sexual charisma. The Who had king-sized egos. "Whiter Shade of Pale" amazed millions of people everywhere. Bob Dylan was a legendary songwriter and Cream were a hot noise for a while.
One's reservations about New Wave are mostly in the shape of "if only" remarks. If only Blondie could play. If only Costello wasn't ugly. If only Johnny Rotten didn't take himself so seriously. If only The Jam and The Clash had singers. If only Chas Jankel hadn't left the Blockheads. If only The B-52s could write hits. If only the Blondie audience could see a B-52s concert and realise the differences between a group whose playing is stunning and one whose playing is feeble. If only the B-52s would become Debbie Harry's backing band.
And if only it wasn't all up to The Police to define what New Wave can mean worldwide. If punk-rock was like The Tour de France, Johnny Rotten was wearing the yellow jersey for the first two years, but now, five years in, Sting is cycling down the Champs Elysees with his arms in the air and is about to be surrounded by more photographers than anyone since Casius Clay beat the bear in '64.
At the moment New Wave is in a phase where singles are good, albums are patchy and concerts are boring. The only good concerts are concerts of greatest hits. It is impossible for a group which has done two albums to go onstage and be as good as Van Morrison or Stevie Wonder, who have fifteen years worth of material to draw on, as well as fifteen years worth of experience onstage.

Most groups do not have enough songs. The Police have eight songs: *Roxanne, So Lonely, Can't Stand Losing You, Bed's Too Big, Message In A Bottle, Walking On The Moon, Don't Stand So Close* and *De Do Do Do,* and they are superb musicians, so they can jam the rest. Ian Dury and the Blockheads have a fair parade of big numbers and can build a show round proven blockbusters. UB40 and The Beat can do the same.
Mostly, you need material. Occasionally, someone like Al Green can go on and do one song for an hour and get away with it but Al Green is a sublime stylist. Just because he breaks the rules and gets away with it doesn't mean anyone else can break the rules. It only means that Al Green is a one-in-a-million performer.
Much as I like great singers, I like groups, and a good group with good songs still gets me off. I know that groups make the whole thing work by the presentation of a collective personality in live performance, but I also know that groups are slow and cumbersome painfully unversatile, and that some musicians hold others back. A group is a prison for its members which is why groups break up to form other groups, which break up to form still more groups.
So Glencoe became Loving Awareness which became The Blockheads, and Brinsley Schwarz split into Nick Lowe and The Rumour. When Nick Lowe stopped gigging, his career took off. Ian Dury only started to put it together as funk with Cockney lyrics with a studio group, not a live group.
At the moment, New Wave is still too new for many of its stars to be comprehensively wealthy, and able to dazzle us with their extravagant life styles. But, to some extent, one élite has been replaced by another. The Mick-Rod-Paul-Eric-Elton aristocracy has, for the younger generation at least, been replaced by the Sting-Debbie-Elvis-Johnny-Ian-Chrissie élite.
Cycles of disillusionment and renewal, exhaustion and energy, will continue as they have always done. Friends fall out or grow away from each other. Musicians are not so different from other people. Acquaintances become friends or partners. Syndromes continue. Tax exile will damage a band whether they have long hair or short hair. The drummer's wife, moaning about him being away from home too much and that it's not fair he earns less than the guitarist-songwriter, will always damage the band.
There is always tension between the singer and the band, and

the answer is usually to let the band do their own album. We read recently that The Blockheads are doing their own album, and that Ian Dury is in Nassau recording with reggae super-sessioneers Sly and Robbie. When the band see the sales figures on their album they will realise that the public do not want music, they want personality.

Response to the music is an individual response. I am not convinced of the value of any one person's opinion about music, even my own. The most important opinion in music is the opinion of the person listening to it. Subjectivity is truth. To some extent at least, each person's ears tell a different story. Last month my ears liked listening to The Teardrop Explodes. My ears said it was bliss compared to The Gang Of Four. My ears don't care what it means, if anything. Julian Cope's voice is so warmly exhilarating. It is a singer's groups, with rhythms and riffs and even the guitar sound tailored to showcase his vocal style, and it works. The other members of the band are embellishment, not competition. We were due a decent singer, after five years of horrible shouting and droning. If Phil Collins produced Teardrop they would be as big as Queen in less time than it takes to say Echo and The Bunnymen.

Long term, it's mostly about good songs and good records. The Police were nothing till *Roxanne.* The Pretenders were nothing till *Brass In Pocket,* although Chrissie did not want it on the album because the guitarist wrote half of it. The Vapors *Turning Japanese* is better than any Jam single, because it has a good vocal.

In the future, British groups will tend to make it by sounding different and American groups will tend to make it by sounding the same. At one time in 1976 Cheap Trick were playing in the Sunset Bowling Alley in Waukesha, Wisconsin, and they sent a plane ticket to ace producer Jack Douglas who had done big albums with Aerosmith and he came and discovered them and that is your typical American success story.

Whereas your typical British success story is a late starter like Costello whose recorded output is perhaps the most perfectly typical illustration of the differences between the British and American approaches. As we've seen, *My Aim Is True* was the demo which became an album and allowed Costello to form a band. *This Years Model* captured the vibrant sound of a great band playing great songs. *Armed Forces* is the same band and the same sound softened and streamlined for mass consumption in USA but *Oliver's Army* was not the smash hit it was in Britain, partly because it contained the words "one white nigger" at a time when Costello was suffering from an avalanche of bad publicity following a bar brawl with Bonnie Bramlett's band, who claimed he was a racist. After that the production of *Get Happy* became rougher, and *Trust* was the sound of a team going stale, desperately in need of a fresh pair of ears.

Success takes time. The heroes of the New Wave did not drop out of the sky in 1977. Debbie Harry was once a waitress at Max's Kansas City. The Stranglers were a trio for ages. Sting, now the champion gladiator of the punk revolution, used to be a fat guy with a beard who played bass in a Newcastle jazzrock band called Last Exit.

It takes a long time to make it. Rod Stewart was 27 when he wrote *Maggie May* and became famous. David Bowie had 11 singles out before *Space Oddity* was a hit. Bowie's success came relatively late, but he was more ready for it when it happened. On the same night that the BBC showed *The Police In The East,* the genial *Evita* lyricist Tim Rice, interviewed Bowie in his hotel room in New York, where he was holding court to the media during the stage production of *The Elephant Man* on Broadway.

Unlike all other British chat show hosts, the genial Tim is never stupid, awkward or embarrassing, and he proved to be a perfect foil for Bowie, who was wonderfully charming, articulate and amusing. On this occasion David Bowie made every other pop star ever seen talking on television seem like a moron. He told how he took the title of *Scary Monsters* off a Kellogs packet, and one of his best remarks was "for someone as grasshoppery as myself." Exactly! This is how Bowie thinks of himself, as a skinny insect who hops from Philly to Berlin to Broadway.

One group had eight names before they called themselves Ultravox and signed to Island and then failed and got dropped, and Gary Numan came along and said he had been influenced by them, and John Foxx had left to do a solo album, which became popular, and the others got Midge Ure in to sing and signed to Chrysalis, who got German ace Connie Plank to make a marvellously shallow album of electronic pop called *Vienna.* The long title track became an unlikely single but went to No 2 in the charts and stayed there for four weeks and sold over 700,000.

So perseverance pays, as long as you realise that being in a group, or managing a group, is a long series of disappointments, illuminated by the occasional small triumph. After all, Ian Dury graduated from singing to two roadies to singing to a nation on TV and radio after struggling for only seven years. When asked by disc-jockey Kid Jensen if he ever hankered for a return to the romance of the boozers, Ian quite forcefully replied: "Pub-rock to me was playing for £16 while punters were sick into your bass drum and changing in a loo of young mandrax addicts."

I have no conclusion for this book. All I know is that life goes on, and musicians are just blokes. If they do a duff album occasionally, it's because they are only human.

People will always write songs and start groups. Every time I open a rock paper there are 50 groups I have never heard of and every time I step outside the house someone gives me a demo cassette. And some of the best guitarists in the country are working in music shops, and when some kid goes in to try out a new guitar, the shop assistant casually picks it up and plays some flawless Roy Buchanan licks and casually says "It's only £750"; the kid is just blown away, and stands there with his mouth hanging open.

Players will go on playing and writers will go on writing songs. Managers will go around telling people their boys are the best thing since The Beatles, and producers will go on producing, and publicists will go on blagging journalists. The telephone is the publicist's best friend, and the hyperbole is his second best friend. The two together are invincible.

As we get older, our favourites get older with us. We like to listen to the same voices, but we also like something new. We know that classic albums are often classics because they are true to their time and place. Just as Van Morrison will never write another *Moondance,* Johnny Rotten will never write another *Bollocks.*

Mostly, life goes on. At any British college or university in the last twenty years you could see a bunch of scruffy students drinking beer, and the girls are wearing jeans and sweaters, and the ones whose Dads have money are wearing lush leather boots, and a few lively lads and lasses dash around organising and entertaining the others and doing publications, which always, always complain about the quality of the "coffee-water" in the Union and carry letters and editorials about the problems of getting decent flats. And, in a room next to the bar, a group is playing, and some drunks are dancing while others watch and talk. It never changes. Except that where before the students played table-football, they now play Space Invaders. And music is played in shops and clubs and at parties. One night you'll walk in and a dozen girls in gold sandals are dancing to *Boogie Oogie Oogie,* and another night you'll walk in and a score of chicks in white cowboy boots are dancing to Kid Creole. And somewhere in South London there is a club in a large first floor room where the disco is superloud and the barmaids have to lean forward quickly, intimately, to put their ears an inch from the punter's mouth to hear him say "Two pints of lager" and downstairs are the loos and the group's dressing room, and on the stairs after the gig a synth player with an arty haircut carries a cassette deck, because, at this level, musicians have to roadie for themselves, and pairs of punters trail in and out of the fish and chip shop over the road, past the locked launderette where a ginger pusscat snoozes on a washing-machine. These scenes never change either.

And one of these kids with the arty haircuts will be a world famous entertainer ten years from now, but of course no-one knows which one.

I'm near the end now and I'm amazed to be finishing almost as fresh as when I started and I'm thinking how other people often write about the horror of facing a blank sheet of paper or about dreaming up a clever remark on the way home from a party. I'm not like that, luckily. I'm never short of a few paragraphs and the only time I can remember being stuck for a remark was one night in New York or Boston when a disgusting little groupie zeroed in and surprised me.

I later realised that American groupies are like those computerised torpedoes which drop from helicopters and seek out enemy submarines unerringly, having been programmed to distinguish them from surface ships, wrecks and shoals of fish. So anyway this girl accosts me in the hotel lift and her opening line is "Hi, you from England? How are Mick Jagger, Mark Bolan, David Bowie and all those other fuckers?" and for the first and only time in my life I was speechless. Back in London I told my pal Doug who said that I should have replied "They're fine, and they send their love."

And that's really my message to the USA, and the rest of the world. We're fine, and we send our love.

" " " " " " "Interview" " " " " " "

So *Anarchy In The UK* was a truly revolutionary moment in pop history?
Yes, it was genuinely new. When I first heard it, I didn't understand it. In my whole life I've only heard two rock records I didn't understand straight away. One was the album Are You Experienced? by The Jimi Hendrix Experience in 1967. The other was Anarchy in 1976. Both were revolutionary.

Why didn't you pretend you were a Pistols fan from day one?
Well, the rest of the book is honest, so why be dishonest about that? Anyway, that's exactly what punk was about, and exactly what Explosion is about. The New Wave was created by the audience. It was the product of the generation gap. The fact that I didn't like Anarchy at first is the central truth of this book. I was part of the inertia.

Is rock an inferior art form?
Yes. Even at its best, rock music is an inferior art form. I have always felt that soccer is the most important unimportant thing in the world, and that rock music is the second most important unimportant thing in the world. Gertrude Stein said that journalism is everything that's less interesting tomorrow than it is today, so where does that leave pop journalism? It is healthier and more enjoyable if we realise that most rock writing is a third-rate discussion of a second-rate art form.

Have you done a lot of research for this book?
Very little. It's not intended to be an encyclopaedia. Research is for scholars. I don't care what other people have written, I'm just trying to put my observations down on paper like a thumb-print, as clearly and readably and accessibly as possible.

Do rock critics write for each other?
I don't know. Ask a rock critic. I always think that rock music is something to chat about rather than something to analyse in print. Danny called me the other day and told me he had seen the Squeeze album cover of East Side Story. He said "It's so awful I've got to warn you about it. Think of the worst sleeve you've ever seen in your life and multiply by ten. They make Rockpile look like futurists!" And we laughed and then talked about something else. Far too much attention is given to rock music. There is far too much writing about it. I'm amazed that the market can support so many pop papers and magazines.

You're sabotaging your role here! What do you want to do if you don't want to be a rock critic?
When I was a kid I wanted to be a writer. I still have hopes. One day I'd like to write something that people could read twice.

Do you read books about rock music yourself?
No. Very rarely. Last one was about four years ago, I was doing a review of Mystery Train by Greil Marcus. A very thoughtful book with lots of good stuff on Sly, The Band and Elvis Presley. On the whole I don't want to read about something I feel so comfortable with. I love rock music and I understand it and I care about it, but I'd rather read Maupassant or some stories by Joyce Carol Oates or re-read some old Nabokov.

What do you hope to achieve by writing this book?
I wanted to see how much could be left out. I wanted to mention as few groups as possible. You wouldn't believe the thought that's gone into what I've left out. I didn't want to mention everybody because it's not a review of the school play. There can never be a definitive book about rock music because it is too miscellaneous and too transient, and the truth about it is a subjective truth, as I've tried to show. Each song and each group can be enjoyed by millions of fans and still mean something slightly different to each person.

What is popular music all about?
It's about Adam's warpaint. It's about ten million young women wanting to meet Sting. It's about taking a cassette of your favourite singles on holiday just in case you get sound-starvation. It's about wondering whether The Beat will have a No. 1 single before Teardrop Explodes have a No. 1 single. It's about Toyah karate-chopping her wedding cake and singing "I wanna be free, I wanna be me!" It's about loads of things. It's even about hearing the Human League's electrodisko single on the radio, and thinking it's got a nice robotic throb and is better than the Kraftwerk new entry Paul Burnett played five minutes ago.

Does rock televise?
Almost never. Television is always five years behind the times and always will be.

Is it because rock is about energy and TV flatters the low-key?
Yes, the more low-key the group, the better they come over. The early acoustic/electric Eagles, Ry Cooder or the first half of a Jackson Browne gig, before he gets into all that absurd rockaboogie. In the mid-Seventies the one thing I really missed when I went to see a group was the sense of seeing someone really knocking themselves out, playing and singing and performing like there is no tomorrow. I'd see Clapton and Wings and think that Eric and Paul were class, but far too comfortable. They were playing and singing so far within themselves that it was ridiculous. Old Wave had become good television. Clapton could do Knocking On Heaven's Door and it would come over well on the small screen; it was so jaunty, so throwaway – the frisky gospel groove of a man almost welcoming death, ready to meet his maker. From our armchairs we could watch our favourite white black cruising into middle age. His band had evolved and distilled their particular fusion of black funk and white rock & roll to the point where it worked on TV, although, obviously, a three-inch mono speaker can never convey the dynamics and classy ensemble surges of that group.

But aren't people sick of turning on the TV and seeing yet another bloke playing the guitar?
I suppose they are. When you have seen a clip of Hendrix at Monterey, everything else is redundant, at least visually. So they started to show us other things like The Group Recording The Album. Taking us behind the scenes. Granada TV did a

" " " " " " Interview " " " " " " "

documentary about Rockpile which achieved the not inconsiderable feat of making modern recording seem even more boring than it really is. It somehow managed to compress months of tedium into 40 minutes.

What about pop videos?
An ideal medium for posers. In the video of Fade To Grey the guy from Visage had purple serpents where his eyebrows should have been. There were a few breakthrough pop videos which influenced others, changed what was expected from a pop video. The Boomtown Rats I Don't Like Mondays was directed by David Mallett, and that was the first time ever that a pop video had the energy level of a good TV commercial.
At the London club, Cabaret Futura when Ashes To Ashes comes on the screen the kids almost get down and kiss the floor. Bowie is still God to arty English kids. A lot of the best videos are done by a consortium of Concorde-tripping directors who service the record business: Mallett, Julien Temple, and an Australian guy called Russell Mulcahy, who has a good formula. He steals a bit of Euro-culture, and shoots on film rather than video, which gives the feel of an art film, with greater depth of field. Using the group as models. So the videos that look most vivacious or atmospheric are just three-minute bastardizations of Antonioni, Visconti, Jancso and Fellini. He did Vienna for Ultravox and Musclebound for Spandau with all those forests and fight scenes. Film is overwhelming, it can make the Lake District look like the steppes. What better amusement than a bunch of posers labouring with picks and ploughs and riding horses? The visual is the message, the glamour of the clothes and the locations.

Who was it said every improvement in communications makes the bore more terrible?

I don't know, but he must have been thinking of Kenny Everett. I'd like to break his back.

What are your pet hates?

Lyric sheets with albums. I'm allergic to actressy singers, and The Clash. I can't tell the difference between Kate Bush and Freddie Mercury. I hate to see a good song acted. And I hate club disc-jockeys who have their turntables totally enclosed in a booth with a sign on the door saying NO ENTRY-NO REQUESTS which might as well be a sign saying I'M GOD! FUCK OFF!

What do you have against The Clash?

They're hopelessly unselfcritical. Having proved for four years that he couldn't sing, Joe Strummer did some rappin' tracks on Sandinista and proved that he can't even talk. The Clash took the punk credo of do-it-yourself to its logical limit: Sandinista is the LP-as-fanzine. A work roughly slapped down, stapled together and which falls apart if you look through it twice. I admit they had me worried for a minute when I first heard The Magnificent Seven on John Peel. I thought they had finally made a record I liked. But then when I got the 1299 I played the instrumental side through first and it was boring. Then I played the vocal side and had to take it off after 90 seconds. They don't use a producer because no producer could stand listening to hour after hour of Strummer's vocals. Still, with any luck The Clash will play permanently in USA where people love them because they think they're the Rolling Stones of the New Wave and the journalists wanna do CTP: Clash Touring Party. A Savage Journey Through America With The Clash Urban Guerrillas. The book of the tour. Well, they're welcome to it. American rock critics and The Clash deserve each other. Whenever I am at Island Studios and I see their album cover on the wall I want to get a hammer and stand on the reception desk and smash Give 'Em Enough Rope to pieces, because it is garbage and does not belong up there alongside good albums by Roxy Music and Bob Marley.

Surely each writer is biased?

Of course, but as English soccer manager, Brian Clough (my hero) says "It's only opinion. It makes the world go round". I don't pretend that Explosion is a balanced book. It doesn't have a chapter on The Jam because I refuse to listen to The Jam until they get a singer. I'm upfront about my biases and attitudes. I have always liked body music and feel music and I have always been comfortable with anything funky and jazzy, but lost with anything arty.

But surely there are many groups which are both funky and arty?

There are now, yes. But for years and years there was only one and they were hip and white and from New York and they were the most professional amateurs ever. The Velvet Underground. And many ultra-professional professionals came later, like Talking Heads.

So your New Wave likes and dislikes are very predictable to anyone who knew you in the mid-seventies?

Yes, I think so. My enjoyment of rock music is visceral, sensory, impressionistic, not cerebral. Its the pulse and the feeling that get me, not the idea. I was into early Kool and the Gang and Electrif Lycanthrope and Rampant Syncopatio, the Little Feat bootlegs, Bob Marley, The Crusaders. Music which was feel-oriented and based on the playing and built up from rhythms and riffs. And most of the stuff I enjoy now is like that: The Beat, Pretenders, Blockheads, UB40, Police.

Do you like big gigs or small gigs?

I love clubs. In the first few months when a good group and their

"Interview"

fans are discovering each other the energy exchange can be magic. In 1980 Stray Cats really were explosively energetic and galvanising. If you were close enough to see the spit flying out of Brian Setzer's mouth and the sweat pouring off his brow and the girl in short shorts tattooed on his arm and you could see whether you preferred the drummer's earring to the bass player's earring, then rock & roll was still exciting.

What is your idea of pop ecstasy?

Debbie and The Police doing I'm gonna be your Number One, Spandau Ballet making silent videos! Actually, my fondest dream would be to flash back in time to catch a couple of shows that I missed, like The Wailers at The Speakeasy. By the time I saw them Peter Tosh and Bunny Wailer had left. The original band had evolved an incredible rapport from years of playing and singing together in Jamaica before any white people had ever heard of them.

What about home-taping?

I think the front-loading cassette deck is replacing the stereo turntable. My guess is that the technologies now available to consumers mean that more and more people are taping from their own albums, and from albums borrowed from friends. And inevitably this process involves a lot of editing. People are selective and often two thirds of an album is discarded immediately. For the last five years I've regarded the act of placing a piece of vinyl on a turntable as a nuisance, an obsolete ritual. Cassettes are a new kind of currency. If it's June in London and you have three tracks of the new UB40 and four tracks from Sly And Robbie Present Taxi and a bit of The Beat and Maladie D'Amour by Kid Creole, then you are in good shape. You can take the C-90 with you in the car and listen to it on the way home from a party at 3 a.m. when you want familiarity and don't want your mellow mood interrupted by DJ spiel or ads or newscasts of murder and assassination.

Is interviewing yourself the ultimate arrogance?

No, filming yourself is. But Renaldo and Clara was great. As Dylan said, if anything, it wasn't long enough. The first two hours flashed past in ten minutes.

What about the cultural impact of youth music?

I really don't know about that. Let someone else write a book about that, I'd read it. Maybe. Because I'm so into rock and funk and reggae in my own way I find it hard to make the imaginative jump into the mind of a typical fan. I never thought for one second that dope and rock music would change the world. And I never felt that amphetamine sulphate and spiky hair would change the world either. Obviously the punk revolution was and is a return to music which has something to say. And it put Ian Dury on telly. But if The Beat think that they can ban the bomb, they are out of their brains. A comment I get a lot from young friends and acquaintances of 19 and 22 is "You're very cynical, aren't you?" and I always say "Yeah, but nobody is born cynical, I've earned my cynicism." They are too young to know that you can't change the world. The rich and powerful are powerful and rich and you can become one of them by playing the guitar, but you can't change the world by playing a guitar. It's been tried, and the attempt can be fun or it can be pain, but it's always just an attempt.

Will New Wave ever completely replace Old Wave?

No, dinosaurs will still have mammoth sales. Queen and Pink Floyd are careerists. But it's worth remembering that New Wave is already bigger than it appears to be. Heavy sales of indie records by new acts over a period of time are not reflected in the national charts. We can only guess at the patterns of people's album-buying habits. Intuitively, I have always felt that UB40 are taking sales off Fleetwood Mac, that some guy who is married and thirty may prefer a third UB40 album to another from the hippies in Hawaii. But you can never know for sure. I used to worry about things like that, but not any more. A few years ago I remember saying that I'd like to hold one last huge festival for all the dinosaurs and like Bad Company and Led Company and Thin Company and the Dead Company on the third day, when the last heavy riff has rocked out over the stoned, muddied hordes, and the helicopter has come to take Status Quo off to another festival in Holland, we could have a giant bonfire of loon pants and Eagles albums and the whole acreage could be transformed into a New Wave Induction Centre where everyone could be ritually re-processed. When they came out of the haircut tent, they would all be issued with a Johnny Rotten poster and a free copy of This Years Model.

What about the future?

It's about good songs and good singles. In the long term the difference between making it and not making it is material, writing it or finding it. The stayers of the Seventies were the writers: Bowie, Marley, even Abba. Super Trouper was their ninth Number One. The best-sounding record on the radio now is Being With You by Smokey Robinson. I was surprised but pleased when it made No. 1.

Do you think good music will ever come back?

Who can say? It's all fashion at the moment. People don't just buy music, they buy images, feelings, attitudes.

What will be the next big thing?

That's easy. The next big thing will be something that's already happened. Ska, romance, rockabilly, it's all revivals. The more things change, the more they stay the same.

" " " " " " Interview " " " " " "

"" 119

USA CLUB DIRECTORY
BOSTON

THE CHANNEL
25 Necco St
Boston, MA 02210
(617) 451-1050

Club opened in 1980, and has operated under the same management since. 8 foot video screen, and 24 speakers for live performance. Dance floor.

Major Bands: Gang of 4, The Stranglers, Steppin' Wolf, The Jam, Joan Jett and the Blackhearts, The Feelies, Joe Cocker, Martha & The Muffins, Robin Lane, The Brains, Dirty Looks, New Riders of the Purple Sage, Edgar Winter, The Plasmatics and Steel Pulse.

On the Rise Bands: The Atlantics, The Dead Kennedys, The Neighbourhood, The Stompers, Private Lightning, The Gogos, The Slits, Human Sexual Response.

THE METRO
15 Lansdown St
Boston, MA 02435
(617) 267-2424

Club opened in 1981, and the management that ran the club while it was the Boston-Boston continued to run it as The Metro. Capacity 1200. Dance floor. 15 foot video screen. 8 JBL speakers.

Major Bands: The Ramones, Adam & The Ants, Southside Johnny & The Ashbury Dukes, Jim Carroll, Iggy Pop and Garland Jeffries.

On the Rise Bands: Primarily play at the Spit, next door and run by the same management.

The Metro is mainly a rock and roll club, but operates as an overflow for the large New Wave performances which cannot fit in to Spit next door. Same owner and manager as the Metro.

THE RAT
528 Commonwealth Ave.,
Boston, MA 02215
(617) 267-4156

Club opened in 1975, and has operated under the same management since then. Capacity 250. Dance floor. 5 monitor video system.

Major Bands: The Jam, The Cars, The Stranglers, Talking Heads, The Runaways, The Damned, Blondie, The Dead Boys, The Ramones, J Giels Band, Gang of Four, Dead Kennedys, The Police, Patti Smith.

On the Rise Bands: City Thrills, The New Models, Someone & The Somebodies, The Outlets and Lou Miami & The Cosmetics.

Again a club from which many success stories started. The Rat has never compromised into more commercial forms of music such as rock disco.

SPIT
13 Landsdowne St
Boston, MA 02435
(617) 262-2457

Opened in 1980, has been under the same management since. Capacity 600. 6 foot video screen, and 4 video monitors. 8 monitors will be operating soon in what will be a video lounge. 8 JBL speakers. Dance floor.

Major Bands: The Vapors, B-52s, English Beat, U-2, The Simple Minds, The Fall, Sad Gadget, Bush-Tetras, Brian Brain, Delta-5, The Shirts, The Waitresses, The Modettes and Romeo Void.

Only exclusively New Wave club in Boston. Features local On the Rise Bands.

CHICAGO

GASPAR'S
3159 North Southport
Chicago, IL 60657
(312) 871-6680

Club opened in 1976. Has operated under present management since 1977. Capacity 350. Dance floor.

Major Bands: Ultravox, 999, The Shirts, Mitch Rider, Dave Wagner & Crow, Daevid Allen with Planet Gang, Pierre Morelen, The Romantics, Max Romeo & The Upsetters and John Cale among others.

On the Rise Bands: Fill in the Blanks, Poison Squirrel, Heavy Manors, The Odd Singles and BB Spin.

Gaspar's is the restored location of the old Schlitz Beer brewery, retaining the old architecture. Lots of wood and glass. Present management made it a music club. Had been a bar previously.

HOLIDAY BALLROOM
4847 N. Milwaukee
hicago, IL 60630
(312) 283-9040

Club will open July 1981. Will have dance floor and video.

A major promoter in Chicago is putting together the list of acts that will appear here. Will feature major New Wave bands with recording contracts as well as On the Rise Bands.

MISFITS
6459 North Sheridan Road
Chicago, IL 60626
(312) 465-4063

Club opened in May 1981. Capacity 450. Dance floor. Bag-end Sound System.

Major Bands: Shrapnel, The Fast, X, Insect Surfers and The Effigies.

On the Rise Bands: The Reason.

Only New Wave club on the North Side of Chicago.

O'BANION'S
661 N. Clark
Chicago, IL 60610
(312) 664-8585

Club opened in July 1978 and has been under the same management ever since. Capacity 600. Dance floor.

Major Bands: Clark's, Strike Under, Meaty Buys and Adrienne, among others.

On the Rise Bands: Bohemia, Fill in the Blanks, Heavy Manors.

O'Banion's is a renovated speakeasy from Chicago's gangster days. It features live bands on Monday and Thursday nights, and a DJ seven nights.

PARK WEST
322 West Armitage
Chicago, IL 60614
(312) 929-1322

Club opened in 1977 and has been under the same management ever since. Holds 750 people in concert, and over 1000 in standing/party situations. Dance floor. Shows both 16mm and 35mm films and has 5 video screens, ranging from 10 by 12ft to 25 by 40ft.

Major Bands: Dave Mason, The Pretenders, Angel City, Pyschedelic Furs, Steve Forbet, English Beat, Dire Straits, The B-52s, The Jam, XTC, The Ramones, Buzzcocks, 999, Lou Reed, Iggy Pop and Ultravox.

On the Rise Bands: Billy Squire, Dennis Brown.

Diverse groups perform there — from reggae, to New Wave, to rock and roll.

TUTS
959 West Belmont
Chicago, IL 60657
(312) 477-3365

Club opened in 1980 under present management. Capacity 500. Dance floor. Occasional video. Powerful sound system.

Major Bands: Magazine, The Cramps, Capt. Beefheart, Joe King Carrasco, Jim Carroll Band, Klaus Nomi, William Burrow, Rockettes, Bust Boys, Echo & The

Bunnymen, Martha & The Muffins, Pere Ubu, Mitch Rider, Ronny Spector, Glenn Matlock & Spectre, Human Sexual Response, The Waitresses, The Pirates and Wasmo Mariz, among others.

On the Rise Bands: Desmond, BB Spin, Lasmo and Tut.

Tuts features bands from the regional as well as national circuit. One of the managers is former MC from CBGBs.

LOS ANGELES

GAZARRI'S
9039 Sunset Blvd.
Los Angeles, CA 90069
(213) 273-6606

Club opened in 1960, and has been under the same management ever since. Capacity 350. Dance floor. Has had video since 1968. Camera and spots, so performances can be shown on TV monitors around club as they are happening.

Major Bands: The Motels, Plimsouls, The Gogos, The King Bees, The Rolling Clones, The Outlaws, Phil Seymour, Martha & The Muffins, among many others.

Gazarri's has been a premier rock club in Los Angeles since it opened. Many top performers have played here including Led Zeppelin, Sonny & Cher, Redbone, The Righteous Brothers and Pete Wilcox. Perhaps most noteworthy performer is Elvis Presley. Gazarri's is also reputed to be the first club where The Doors played. The film "The Idolmaker" was filmed in Gazzarri's as is the TV series "Hollywood Heartbeat" starring Blondie. Each year Gazarri's sponsors a renowned Ladie's Dance Contest. past winners include Barbi Benton (1968) and Katherine Bach (1974). Gazzari's has a cooperative relationship with KMET Radio in Los Angeles, who broadcast many Gazarri's acts live.

THE ON KLUB
3037 Sunset Blvd.
Los Angeles, CA
(213) 665-1286

Club opened under present management in 1980. Capacity 100. Dance floor. Acts often provide video.

Major Bands: The Raybeats, The Fabulous Thunderbirds, DNA, Lydia Lunch and The Babylonian Warriors.

On the Rise Bands: The Box Boys, The Rebel Rockers, The Hoovers and Skachacha.

Primary focus is on ska and reggae, with New Wave during the week.

THE ROXY
9009 Sunset Blvd.
Los Angeles, CA 90069
(213) 878-2222

Club opened in September 1973 under present management. Capacity 450. Dance floor.

Major Bands: Rockpile, The Gogos, The Ramones (1976), The Waitresses, Bruce Springsteen (1975), Bob Marley (1975), David Essex, Patti Smith, Lou Reed, Television, John Cale and Suzie Quatro among others.

The Roxy opened in 1973 to be a major venue for rock and roll bands including Neil Young, Richie Havens, Joe Walsh, The Temptations, Linda Rondstadt, Frank Zappa, Rick Nelson, The Hollies, Smokey Robinson, Jackson Browne, Ravi Shankar and Boz Skaggs among others. Owned and managed by owner/manager of The Whisky.

THE TROUBADOR
9081 Santa Monica
Los Angeles, CA 90069
(213) 276-6168

Club opened in 1957. Has operated under present management since 1979. Capacity 300. Small dance floor. Can record from sound board.

Major Bands: The Textones, Shandi, Naughty Sweeties, 20-20, The Motels, The Gogos, The Humans, The Kats, The Nack, Scooters, John Hyate, UXA, X, Fear, The Alley Kats, Plimsouls, The Weirdos, Ray Camp & The Rockabilly Rebels, Levy & The Rockettes, The Heaters, The Cretones, The Geers, The Cramps, Paul Warren's Explorer and Phil Seymour, among others.

The Troubador has been a major force in the L.A. music scene for many years. Elton John made his major L.A. debut here. Others who have performed here include: Jackson Browne, Eric Burdon, Rita Coolidge, Dion, Tim Hardin, Carol King, Leo Kottke, Gordon Lightfoot, Joni Mitchell and The Everly Brothers, among many others. The Troubador often showcases unknown talent.

THE WHISKY
8901 Sunset Blvd.
Los Angeles, CA 90069
(213) 652-4202

Club opened in 1963 under present management. Capacity 300. Dance floor. Will have video late 1981.

Major Bands: Joplin, The Psychedelic Furs, 999, Gang of Four, Split Enz, The Slits, 77, Squeeze, Joan Jett, John Cale, Dead Boys, Screamers, The Gogos, Tom Robinson, Jim Carroll, Martha & The Muffins, The New York Dolls, Echo & The Bunnymen, Johnny Thunder, Elvis Costello, Devo and David Johanson (1973), among others.

The Whisky is owned and managed by the very people who own and manage The Roxy, right down the street from The Whisky. The Whisky concentrates more on up-and-coming talent while the Roxy deals with major acts. The Whisky introduced Lou Reed to L.A. in 1965. The Whisky was the first L.A. club to feature Elvis Costello. Known as "The Soul of Rock and Roll." During the '60s, The Whisky's house band was The Doors.

NEW ORLEANS

JED'S
88301 Oak Street
New Orleans, LA
(504) 861-2585

Major Bands: The East Cambodians; The Defectors; The Ram Shots.

On the Rise Bands: Red Rockers.

Music was on Tuesday and Thursday nights.

TIPITINA'S
501 Napolean Ave.
New Orleans, LA 70115
(504) 395-7115

Opened in 1977, and has been operating under present management since 1980. Capacity 400. Dance floor. 16 channel board sound system with 6 cabinets.

Major Bands: Doctor John, Albert King, Taj Mahal, Etta Jones and Delbert McClinton.

On the Rise Bands: The Neville Brothers, The Radiators and Little Queenie & The Percolators.

The club was started by Professor Longhair, who used to perform there often.

NEW YORK

BONDS
Broadway at 45th St.
New York, NY
(212) 944-5880

Capacity 1,700. Huge dance floor. Video equipment. Mixed sound system.

Major Bands: The Clash, Selecter, Gary Glitter, Soft White Underbelly, The Stranglers, The Contortions, Plasmatics, Blotto, Catholic Girls, Dead

Kennedys, Flesh Tones, Our Daughter's Wedding, Certain Generals.

On the Rise Bands: The Sleepers, Urban Blight, Strange Party, The Must, Shrapnel, The Hard, Bel-byzantens.

Converted from the old Bond International building. Bond International used to be the largest clothing department store in the world. The building is a Times Square fixture. Club is huge; has enormous rooms and many levels.

THE BOTTOM LINE
15 W. 4th St.
New York, NY 10012
(212)228-6300

Club opened in February 1974 under present management. Capacity 400. Tables and chairs.

Major Bands: Suzie Quatro and The New York Dolls (March 74), Steve Harley & Cockney Rebel (Dec. 75), The Streetwalkers (Dec. 75), Patti Smith (Dec. 75 and other dates), Dr. Feelgood (May 76), The Ramones (May 76), Lou Reed (June 76), Brian Ferry (June 76), Talking Heads (June 76), Dwight Twilley (Nov. 76), Tom Petty (Nov. 77), Hawkwind (78), Ian Dury (78), The Rockettes (78), Nick Lowe & Rockpile (78), Television (78), Cheap Trick (78), Tom Robinson (June 78), David Johanson (July 78), Tin Huey (Aug. 78), Flamin' Groovies (Aug. 78), Gregg Kihn Band (Aug. 78), Tim Curry (Oct. 78), Devo (Oct. 78), also 1978: The Be Stiff Tour, Reckless Eric, Jona Lewie, Lene Lovich, Rachel Sweet, The Records and Elvis Costello. In 1979: The Police, Joe Jackson, Squeeze, Herman Brood & His Wild Romance, The Records, Ian Gomm, The Yachts, Lou Reed. In 1980: The Inmates, The Romantics, The Rattlers, John Cale, The Tourists, Squeeze, Dirty Looks, The Brains, The Jags, Magazine, Jim Carroll, The Plimsouls, The Blasters, Buzz & The Flyers, The Plastics, Sil Sylvane and The Lounge Lizards, among others.

The Bottom Line is one of New York's top music clubs. The club features a wide variety of music and a spectrum of styles from jazz to blues to rock to punk to new wave. Many bands have made their "major" New York club debuts in the Bottom Line, including Patti Smith and Talking Heads.

CAMOUFLAGE
38 Dell Boulevarde
Bayside, Queens 11361 (NY)
(212) 631-7656

Opened in 1980 and has been run by the same management since. Capacity 200. Dance floor. 6 monitor video system. PA system and separate dance speakers.

Major Bands: Blue Angel, Joan Jett & the Blackhearts, The Shirts, Blotto, The Raybeats and Our Daughter's Wedding.

On the Rise Bands: Cheverne, Hooks, Vogue, Thin Ice and Wayne Cramer.

CBGBs
315 Bowery
New York, NY 10003
(222) 473-9763

Club opened in 1973 under present management. Capacity 350. Dance floor. 16 track recording facilities.

Major Bands: Blondie, Television, Talking Heads, The Ramones, Patti Smith, Mink de Ville, Tough Darts, The Shirts, Lenny K, Laughing Dogs, Dead Boys, Tom Petty & the Heartbreakers, Wire, Police, Squeeze, XTC, The Jam, Cooper, The Runaways, Steve Forbert, The Waitresses, The Pet Clams, B-52s, Devo, John Cale, Nico, Suicide & The Heartbreakers, The Plasmatics and many others.

On the Rise Bands: The Nightcaps, The Revlons, Joe Marshall, Urban Blight, The Sick Fucks and The Drongos.

CBGBs was New York's first punk club. Many of the early punk bands got their start here, including Blondie, Plasmatics, Patti Smith, and the launching of John Cale's second career. The Ramones played CBs long before they went to the U.K. with Seymour Stein and kicked it all open. Five months after that, the Sex Pistols burst on the scene in a major way.

CLUB 57
17 Irving Plaza
New York, NY 10003
(212) 477-5030

Club opened in 1978, and has operated under the present management since 1979. Capacity 800. 18 speakers. Dance floor.

Major Bands: B-52s, The Gang of Four, Buzzcocks, Siouxsie & the Banshees, Iggy Pop, The Ramones, Talking Heads, James Brown, Robert Fripp, XTC, Pere Ubu, Magazine, Captain Beefheart, Psychedelic Furs.

On the Rise Bands: Bush-Tetras, Dead Kennedys, Fad Gadget, Circle Jerks, Black Flag, the Actors, The Waitresses and DNA.

THE LEFT BANK
20 E. 1st St
Mt. Vernon, NY 105500
(914) 699-6619

Opened in 1980, and has operated under the same management since. Capacity 800. Nine monitor video, 24 track sound board. 8 speaker cabinets. Dance floor.

Major Bands: James Brown, Plasmatics, Plastics, The Vapours, Robert Gordon, Sam & Dave, Mink De Ville, Doug & the Slugs, Screamin' Jay Hawkins, Gang of Four, 999, Fleshtones, NRBQ and The Dictators.

On the Rise Bands: David Leonard & The Look, Hello, the Catholic Girls and Cheap Perfume.

MAX'S KANSAS CITY
213 Park Ave. South
NY 10010

Club opened in 1964. Has operated under present management since 1975. Capacity 250. Limited dance space. 4 monitor video system. 2 stacks of speakers, 2000 watts each.

Major Bands: The Heartbreakers, Dead Kennedys, Troggs, The Stray Cats, James Chance & The Contortions, Patti Smith, Blondie, The Ramones, Bob Marley, Bachman Turner Overdrive, The Stooges, Bruce Springsteen.

On the Rise Bands: Von Lmo, The Senders, The Stimulators, Bad Brains, The False Prophets and The Drongos.

Max's Kansas City was a major rock club in the 60s, featuring many of the top rock bands of the 60s (and giving many up and coming 60s bands a chance to establish themselves). The club was reopened in 1975 to provide a venue for the punk and new wave bands of the late 70s.

THE MUDD CLUB
77 White St.
New York, NY
(212) 227-7777

Club opened in 1978 under present management. Capacity 250. Videos shown on monitors throughout club.

Major Bands: Talking Heads, Joe Johnson, Frank Zappa, Madness, B-52s, 999, Our Daughter's Wedding, Bushtetras, Psychedelic Furs, Raybeats, among many others.

The Mudd Club is more than just a music club. It is known nationally for the various special events it sponsors (particularly on fashion), and also presents live theatre. The club's special events get more press than the music, although it's known for its musical tastes among those who frequent New York clubs. The club also specializes in revivals of old rock and rhythm and blues acts, such as: The Ventures, Sam & Dave, The Shirelles, The Marvellettes, Clarence Carter, Joe Tex and others.

MY FATHER'S PLACE
19 Bryant Ave.
Roslyn, NY 11574
(516) 621-8700

Club opened in 1971 under present management. Capacity 550. Dance floor.

Video on advent white screen.

Major Bands: Kid Creole & the Coconuts, Gang of Four, Bruce Springsteen, Joan Jett & the Blackhearts, Psychedelic Furs, Jonathan Richman, The Slits, Robert Gordon, David Johanson, Steel Pulse, UB40, Police and The Drongos, among others.

My Father's Place is also a major east coast venue for reggae music. The club also showcases comedy acts, blues, jazz and folk music.

THE PEPPERMINT LOUNGE
128 W. 45th St.
New York, NY 10036
(222) 719-3141

Club re-opened in 1980 under present management. Capacity 542. Two dance floors. 15-20 video monitors throughout the club.

Major Bands: Madness, Echo & the Bunnymen, Talking Heads, 999, Bushtetras, The Bongos, Syl Sylvane, David Johanson, X, The Gogos, Joan Jett, Urban Verb, Inner Circle, Plastics, Ronny Spector, Richard Hell & the Voidoiss, Martha & The Muffins, The Rockettes, Joe King Carrasco and Curtis Lowe, among others.

The original Peppermint Lounge opened in 1960, and was the "Home of the Twist". The Twist was born in the Peppermint Lounge. The club has been through a lot of changes since then. Then, in 1980, the present management took over, changed the name back to its original, The Peppermint Lounge, and are filling it with rock and new wave music.

PRIVATES
150 E. 85th
New York, NY 10028
(212) 744-9382

Club opened in 1980 under present management. Capacity 900. Dance floors on 1st and 3rd floors. Show 16mm films.

Major Bands: Madness, 999, Joan Jett & The Blackhearts, The Stranglers, Stiff Little Fingers, XTC, The Cramps, Sam & Dave, Chubby Checker, Ronnie Spector, Teardrop Explodes, Steel Pulse, Delta 5, John Cale, Richard Lloyd, Blue Angel, Eddie & The Hot Rods, Willy Nile, The Revillos, Joe King Carrasco, Bauhause, Bo Diddley, Four Tops, Hazel O'Connor, The Members and The Spectres.

Privates is a renovated old German social hall, which looks like a Bavarian Beer Hall. Lots of wood makes good acoustics.

THE RITZ
119 E. 11th St.
New York, NY 10003
(212) 254-2800

Club opened May 1980 under present management. Capacity 1,000. Huge dance floor. 15 x 20ft video screen. Independent sound systems upstairs and downstairs.

Major Bands: 999, Gang of Four, Pretenders. Rockpile, Jerry Lee Lewis, Gladys Knight, Squeeze, Jimmy Cliff, Split Enz, Robert Gordon, Chuck Berry, Gary US Bonds, Jam, Tina Turner, Garland Jeffries, John Cale, Adam & The Ants, Steve Forbert, Ray Charles, Jim Carroll and the Psychedelic Furs among others.

On the Rise Bands: The Drongos, Our Daughter's Wedding, Get Wet, Robin Lane & The Chart Busters and The Rockets, among others.

TRAX
10 W. 72nd St.
New York, NY 10023
(212) 799-1554

Club opened in 1976. Has operated under present management since 1979. Capacity 280. Dance floor. 6ft video screen.

Major Bands: Chris Spedding, Stiff Little Fingers, Average White Band, Eve Moon, The Waitresses, Nervous Wrecks, Mona Hendricks, The Plimsouls, Lounge Lizards, The Fools, Mink de Ville, Steve Forbert, Billy Burnett, Jim Carroll, The Shirts, The Psychedelic Furs, The Elevators, Blotto, The Vapors, Huey Lewis & The News, Get Wet, The Brains, Kid Creole & the Coconuts

and Gary US Bonds.

On the Rise Bands: The Drongos.

Trax is the only New Wave club on the upper west side of Manhattan. They have done a number of live broadcasts on WPIX radio.

SAN FRANCISCO

THE BERKELEY SQUARE
1333 University Ave.
Berkeley, CA 94702
(415) 849-3374

Club opened in 1980 under present management. Capacity 300. Dance floor. Soon installing a video system. 5 speakers for monitors, 6 for PA.

Major Bands: Hostages, John Cale, Plastics, Jim Carroll, The Raybeats, James Chance & The Contortions.

On the Rise Bands: SVT, No Sisters, The Lloyds, The Mutants, Bushtetras.

THE KEYSTONE PALO ALTO
260 California
Palo Alto, CA 94306
(415) 324-1402

Club opened in 1977 under present management. Capacity 800. Dance floor.

Major Bands: All those listed for The Stone in San Francisco, plus Gang of Four and Secret Affair.

THE KEYSTONE BERKELEY
2119 University Ave.
Berkeley, CA 94704
(415) 841-9903

Club opened in 1970 under present management. Capacity 800. Dance floor.

Major Bands: Same as The Stone and the Keystone Palo Alto.

THE MABUHAY GARDENS
443 Broadway
San Francisco, CA 94133
(415) 956-3315

Club opened in 1972 under present management. Capacity 235. Dance floor. Video and 16mm films.

Major Bands: Blondie, The Ramones, The Dictators, Devo, The Jam, Madness, The Damned, Matchbox, Dead Kennedys, SVT, Victims, and DOA, among others.

The Mabuhay Gardens started out as a Philipino ethnic supper club, and in 1976, opened it's doors to Punk bands — the first and (for a while) only place in San Francisco the punks could play. A restaurant in the day time, the Mabuhay offers theatre from 8:30 to 10:30. There are three bands a night, seven nights a week here. Dead Kennedys got their start here.

THE OLD WALDORF
444 Battery St.
San Francisco, CA 94111'
(415) 397-4335

Club opened in 1977. Has operated under present management since 1980. Capacity 600. Dance floor.

Major Bands: The Plastics, John Cale, U2, Gary US Bonds, Jefferson Starship, Garland Jeffries, Teardrop Explodes, Echo & The Bunnymen, Joe King Carrasco, Tuxeco Moon, The Gogos, Capt. Beefheart, Jim Carroll, The Bust Boys, Split Enz, English Beat, Lou Reed, Modettes, The Motels, The Jags and Selecter, among others.

On the Rise Bands: SVT, Eye Protection, DOA and DNA.

The Old Waldorf mainly features touring bands who are attached to record companies. They do book non-New Wave bands as well, including rock and jazz.

THE SOUND OF MUSIC
162 Turk St.
San Francisco, CA 94102
(415) 885-9616

Club opened in June 1978 under present management. Capacity 150. Giant 50 inch video monitor. Dance floor.

Major Bands: Dead Kennedys, DOA, The Offs, The Indoor Life, Lloyd, The Slippers, and Big Boys, among others.

On the Rise Bands: Nervous Gender, Wolvaurines, Hostages, Undersong, and The Explosion, among others.

The Sound of Music specializes in featuring unknown bands. They have live music seven nights a week, and often have as many as five bands play in a night.

THE STONE
412 Broadway
San Francisco, CA 94133
(415) 391-8282

Club opened in 1980 under present management. Capacity 700. Dance floor. Two 4 x 4ft video screens. Concert PA system.

Major Bands: Ultravox, James Brown, The Slits, Stranglers, Martha & The Muffins, Plasmatics, Rough Trade Acts (all of them), XTC, Jim Carroll, Culture, Capt. Beefheart, James Blood Ulmer, James Chance & The Contortions, The Feelies, Chris Spedding, Tom Robinson & Sector 27, Joan Jett, Steel Pulse, Johnny Thunder & The Heartbreakers, The Undertones, UB40, The Cramps, 999, Sam & Dave, Ray Charles, Big Youth, The Vapors, Orchestral Manoeuvres in the Dark, and others.

On the Rise Bands: The Gregg Kihn Band, Huey Lewis & The News, The Ventures, The Off, Our Daughter's Wedding, Lee Perry, SVT, The Mutants and Dennis Brown.

The Stone is part of the Keystone Family of clubs (Keystone Berkeley and Keystone Palo Alto are others). The Keystone family clubs do a lot of experimental stuff and like to feature new music and new bands. Most bands play all three clubs. The owners of the Stone used to own The Keystone Corner, San Francisco's major jazz club. The site of the present Stone is on the old Matrix, which was the first place Bob Marley played in San Francisco.

TEXAS

THE AGORA
5134 Richmond
Houston, TX
(713) 960-1318

Major Bands: The Cheaters, Tuse Newton, Billy Squire, The Lounge Lizards, The Sheiks, Pandora, Phil Silvane & The Teardrops, Alistair Hailey, True Hearts and the Bombers.

Concerts produced by Pace Concerts.

CLUB FOOT
110 F. 4th St.
Austin, TX 78701
(512) 472-4345

Club opened in August 1980 and has operated under same management since. Capacity 1,000. Dance floor. Will have video late fall 1981. 24 bias board sound system.

Major Bands: Delbert McClinton, Sam & Dave, James Brown, Juici Newton, The Thunderbirds, Joe King Carrasco, The Skunks and Grace Jones among others.

On the Rise Bands: D-day and Five Spot.

Club Foot is a large club with three levels, three bars, large stage and a cat walk. A new club that is still evolving and changing.

THE CONTINENTAL CLUB
135 Congress
Austin, TX 78701
(512) 442-9904

Club opened in 1963. Has operated under present management since August 1980. Capacity 100. Dance floor. Television.

Major Bands: Rocky Erikson with the Explosives, Al Cooper, Butch Hancock, Alistair Hailey, Joe Healy, Doug Sahn, The Cobras, among others.

On the Rise Bands: D-Day and The Bats.

The Continental Club was Austin's first topless nightclub when it opened in 1963. Later, it was Austin's premier pool palace. The current management took over in 1980 and turned it into a rock club, with bands seven nights a week.

DUKE'S ROYAL COACH
318 N. Congress
Austin, TX 78701
(512) 472-0321

Club opened in 1968, and has been under the same management since. Capacity 300. Dance floor. Occasional 16mm films.

Major Bands: The Stairs, Joe King Carrasco, The Offenders, The Dicks and The Big Boys, among others.

On the Rise Bands: Rank & File.

Duke's Royal Coach started out as a Mexican club, featuring only Mexican music. In 1976 Joe King Carrasco (who was then in a Mexican band who frequently played Duke's) decided to try something musically different. Neither the Club, nor Joe, has been the same since. Joe King Carrasco is a major New Wave performer and Duke's is one of the premier New Wave clubs in Texas.

THE HOT CLUB
4350 Maple
Dallas, TX
(214) 526-9432

Major Bands: Red Tape, Bag of Water & The Ralph, Irving Berg & The Mentals, The Telephones, Romeo Boid and The Fall.

TORONTO

THE EL MOCAMBO
464 Spadina Ave.
Toronto, Canada M57 2G8
(416) 961-2558

Club opened in 1972. has operated under present management since 1976. Capacity 450 (150 downstairs; 300 upstairs). Dance floor.

Major Bands: The Ventures, The Glass, U2, The Vapors, The Inmates, Jim Carroll, The Models, Blondie, Lounge Lizards, Rough Trade, Joan Jett, The Understones, Garland Jeffries, The Ramones, The Damned, The Poles, The Runaways, Tom Robinson and Elvis Costello, among others.

On the Rise Bands: The Battered Wives.

Also feature bands outside the Punk/New Wave genre, such as Graham Parker, and Southside Johnny. The Rolling Stones recorded their album "Love You Live" at The El Mocambo in 1977.

STUDIO 167
167 Church St.
Toronto, Ontario
Canada
(416) 364-7509

Reggae and New Wave.

LONDON CLUB DIRECTORY

BILLY'S (Now closed)

Capacity: 100+

Based in the former premises of a dubious Soho 'club', at the corner of Wardour and Beak Streets, Billy's was founded by former Rich Kids drummer and Visage sticks man, Rusty Egan. Egan, and Visage mainman, Steve Strange, used Billy's as the testing ground for their electro-funk disco, which many claim was the instigation for the subsequent New Romantic and Futurist movements. In its short life (roughly six months from the winter of 1979) the club played a crucial role in the development of many budding futurist musicians like Gary Kemp of Spandau Ballet, Egan and Strange of Visage and many of the post-punk dance bands that played there, notably Killing Joke.

BLITZ (Nightclub)
4 Great Queen Street, WC2
01-405 6598

Capacity: 200+

Not a music club, like the Marquee, but a bastion of the style and pose conscious New Romantics and Futurists, Blitz opened in 1978 as a tasteful, unpretentious cocktail bar, restaurant and nightclub. The management encouraged a clientele that enjoyed the stylishness and theatrical consciousness that led to the New Romantic movement which, under the spell of house deejay and guiding light, Steve Strange made the Blitz its first headquarters. The club's early offbeat cabaret entertainments were a direct pre-cursor of the later alternative cabaret scene. Music is usually furnished by a guest or house deejay — unorthodox disco and dance music — supplemented by live acts.

BRIDGE HOUSE (Pub)
Barking Road, Canning Town, E16
01-476 2889

Capacity: 300+

Since the early 70s, and in a more irregular manner before that, the east London pub has provided a staple part of the city's club circuit. In recent years The Bridge House has contributed mostly to the development of 'local' punk and skinhead bands like The Cockney Rejects, The Four Skins and The Business, although most bands play the place on the way up. Frequently local heavies visit the bar just prior to closing time and stay for after hours drinks and the pub's tough neighbourhood did at one time give The Bridge House an unfair reputation for crowd violence.

CABARET FUTURA (Nightclub)
13 Wardour Street, W1
01-677 4085

Capacity: 150+

Established in early 1981 by musician and event merchant, Richard Strange, Cabaret Futura has established itself at the Latin Quarter club as the regular home of those 'fringe' or alternative comedy, poetry music and performance acts branded alternative cabaret. Like Blitz it acts more as a sort of imput into a scene rather than as a music club. The bands that provide the live music at Cabaret Futura are usually the more unusual, experimental bands that don't easily fit in elsewhere like the staggering, post punk barber shop quartet, Furious Pig and Strange himself.

DINGWALLS (Nightclub)
Camden Lock, Chalk Farm Road, NW1
01-267 4967

Capacity: 400+

Although snubbed by the hard core punk and new wave bands — The Sex Pistols and The Clash refused to play there — almost all the major (and minor) bands have played at London's oldest (it opened in 1974) surviving (since the Speakeasy closed) rock nightclub. Dingwalls has successfully kept pace with developing musical trends and despite its 'groovy' music biz image, it managed to attract the punk/new wave audience and had enormous success with The Damned, The Slits, Blondie and many others. With an extensive video system and a (of late) once again more varied booking policy, the club is successfully catering for the wide variety of new bands on the scene and has contributed to the rise of Toyah, The Stray Cats and The Belle Stars.

GREYHOUND (Pub)
175 Fulham Palace Road, W6
01-385 0526

Capacity: 472 (!)

A fairly typical example of the larger London pub venue, the Greyhound has operated a 'live music policy' since the 60s achieving prominence with the pub-rock boom of 1973-1975. Like most of the pub circuit it succumbed to the economic reality of punk and slowly gave over to booking new wave acts early in 1977. The dancehall area was rebuilt in 1978 and Tracy Lee (partner of pub booking agent Jazz Summers) took over booking and a healthy new wave etc. policy has been developed. Up and coming bands have traditionally played there as an established part of the circuit, but they usually quickly leave it behind. The pub enjoyed a strong involvement in the 1979 Mod revival and 2 Tone band The Specials played their last London pub gig there.

ELECTRIC BALLROOM (Now a roller disco)
Chalk Farm Road, NW1

Capacity: 1500+

Built in the pre World War II British ballroom dancing boom, the building that housed the Electric Ballroom survived as a social mecca for the local Irish community. It was taken over in 1978 by promoter John Curd who introduced punk and new wave bands to the venue. During its erratic two-year lifespan it played host to a broad cross-section of developing new wave talent including Adam & The Ants, Siouxsie & The Banshees, The Ramones, The Human League, a solo Sid Vicious, The B52s, The Gang Of Four and a host of others. It is currently a successful roller skate disco.

HAMMERSMITH PALAIS (Ballroom)
242 Shepherds Bush Road, W6
01-748 2812

Capacity: 3000+

The Hammersmith Palais, like The Electric Ballroom and the Lyceum, was built during the 1930s and continued as a major dance hall up until the beginning of the 70s when it began to be used for major rock concerts. Its role as a new wave venue was instigated by The Clash, who refused to play venues where the audience was forced to remain seated and selected The Palais for their major London date in 1977. In The Clash's wake The Pretenders, Elvis Costello, The Specials, Madness, Kraftwerk and hundreds more bands have chosen to headline at the Palais. John Curd's Straight Music organisation is the main promoter for the venue.

HOPE & ANCHOR (Pub)
207 Upper Street, Islington, N1
01-359 4510

Capacity: 100+

The tiny basement of the Hope & Anchor — London's most famous pub-rock (1973-1975) transformed it into one of the top five such venues in the capital. It was at the end of the pub-rock period that John Eichler and his wife Sue took the place over and it is fair to say that (bar The Clash and The Sex Pistols) virtually every band that has risen to prominence from pub-rock, punk and new wave has played there — The Damned, The Jam, The Stranglers, The Boomtown Rats, The Police, Elvis Costello, Dave Edmunds, Dire Straits, Madness, The Stray Cats and hundreds of others have trod the tiny stage. Like the Marquee Club, 'The Hope' has become a major rock tourist attraction and bands travel the length of the country to play there.

100 CLUB (Club)
100 Oxford Street, W1
01-636 0933

Capacity: 300+

One of the early 60s London jazz clubs, the 100 Club has a similar, though less-continuous history along the lines of The Marquee. Ahead of all the other venues the 100 Club had the foresight to give The Sex Pistols a residency (from 30 March 1976) and it also provided the location for the two-day New Wave Festival in late September 1976, for which the club's promoter, Ron Lesley, booked The Sex Pistols, The Clash, The Damned, Siouxsie & The Banshees, The Buzzcocks, The Vibrators, The Subway Sect and French group The Stinky Toys to play. It was the second of these two nights that a leading rock journalist was beaten with a chain by Sid Vicious. The 100 Club went on to a varied policy of new wave nights, reggae nights and jazz nights, a policy that survives today.

101 CLUB (Club)
101 St. John's Hill, SW11
01-223 8309

Capacity: 300

Fostered by pioneering radio deejay Charlie Gillett as an outlet for his south London based Oval record label, the 101 Club opened on the site of a disused ballroom dancing school in 1979, and easily established itself as the hip place to play south of the River Thames. Much needed improvements carried out in 1980, following the arrival of a new management team, have certainly made it a more comfortable place to play. Under the club's auspices five albums have been released featuring many of the bands that have played there since the summer of 1980.

THE LYCEUM (Ballroom)
Wellington Street, The Strand, WC2
01-836 3715

Capacity: 2750+

The Lyceum is yet another monument to London's ballroom dancing past, dating back to the 1930s, it has followed a very similar course to The Hammersmith Palais. The venue can record major rock concerts back to the late 60s, but probably the earliest New Wave event occurred when The Sex Pistols supported BOF/rock band The Pretty Things there in July 1976. Since then, virtually all the major New Wave acts have headlined at the Lyceum including Adam & The Ants, The Talking Heads, The Human League, Toyah, The Specials, Kraftwerk, The Damned, The Police, The Slits, etc., etc. Once again the regular Sunday concerts at the Lyceum are promoted by John Curd's Straight Music Company.

THE MARQUEE (Club)
90 Wardour Street, W1
01-437 6603

Capacity: 400+

The Marquee has existed since the early 60s when it operated as a blues and jazz club. It is undoubtedly the most famous club in Europe (excluding Liverpool's now-vanished Cavern and Hamburg's Star Club) for its contribution to the development of rock music for almost twenty years. The clubs astute booking policy, which helped to set trends throughout the 60s and 70s, was rather reluctant to include New Wave following their banning of the Sex Pistols in March 1976 for fighting on stage. It wasn't until the end of 1976/early 1977 that bands like Generation X, Chelsea and The Stranglers were seen regularly there. Again almost all the notable bands (with the exception of The Clash) have played The Marquee, but the club's 60s mod and r'n'b heritage seems to have particularly favoured Eddie & The Hot Rods, The Vibrators and, to an enormously greater degree, The Jam who've played historic, solidly sold-out weekend shows. The Marquee has survived all the trends, tackling Mod (twice), New Wave, Heavy Metal, Rockabilly and Futurist crowds and operates a varied week's schedule drawn from all areas of rock.

MOONLIGHT CLUB/(STARLIGHT) (Clubs)
100 West End Lane, NW6
01-624 7611

Capacity: 250/(200)

The Moonlight Club is attached to the Railway Hotel, the West Hampstead pub that in the mid to late 60s housed the Klooks Kleek r'n'b/rock club. It opened to new wave music in 1978 with mostly rising and second division bands of the time like The Members and Adam & The Ants. The club became The Moonlight when manager Dave Kitson took over in 1979 and the place has maintained an alert booking policy from the tailend of punk, through 2Tone, to the Futuristic bands. The Specials played their first London headline gig at the Moonlight and a famous bootleg recording of one of their later gigs was recorded there.
The smaller Starlight, is situated upstairs from the Moonlight, it opened in 1981 and operates on a very similar basis to its partner enterprise.

MUSIC MACHINE (Now closed)
Camden High Street, NW1

Capacity: 2000+

Basically a smaller, grubbier version of The Lyceum, The Music Machine has a history as a ballroom, a nightclub and one of the most notorious punk venues in London. Its atmosphere of decaying mediocrity provided, in 1977, a home of perfect squalor for the blank generation. Gigs by The Clash, Siouxsie & The Banshees, Iggy Pop and more recently Killing Joke and Toyah, were always accompanied by the stereotypical scenes of punk excess – gobbing, fighting, kids passing out in the toilets and hordes of stranded punks trying to bum rides home at 2:00 am in Camden High Street. On the punk nights the Music Machine, at its height in 1978, took on the character of The Vortex, only on a larger scale. there were frequent allegations of brutality being employed by the venue's bouncers, and from when The Specials played there in 1979 the Music Machine went into a decline and closed in 1980 following a fire.

THE NASHVILLE (Now closed)
171 North End Road, W14

Capacity: 300+

The pub which housed The Nashville was closed and sold by the brewery that owned it and it has been empty and unused since late 1980. As its name implies, The Nashville Rooms was a country and western venue located in the largest bar of a West Kensington pub. The early 70s saw a mixed weekly booking policy covering rock, drag and striptease acts. Pub-rock established The Nashville as a leading venue and Dai Davies and Derek Savage (later to become The Stranglers managers) founded the Albion booking agency which exclusively looked after the Hope & Anchor and The Nashville, and they were responsible for the introduction of New Wave to both venues. In 1976, The Nashville provided early gigs for The Sex Pistols, The Vibrators, The Stranglers, The Damned and went on to give exposure to most of the subsequent bands like The Selecter, The Gang Of Four, The Human League, Hazel O'Connor, Toyah, etc.. The Nashville was killed off following numerous complaints of violence, a fire and eventually a police-enforced ban on the admission of under-20 year olds.

THE RAINBOW THEATRE/RAINBOW UPSTAIRS/RAINBOW DOWNSTAIRS
(Theatre/club/club)
232 Seven Sisters Road, Finsbury Park, N4
01-263 3148

Capacity: 4000/1000/1000

Originally opened in the 1930s as a variety theatre, the Finsbury Park Astoria (as it was then known) was little used after the mid-50s. Following the Beatles Christmas Shows in 1964 it experienced a modest revival as a pop music venue and had a major relaunch as London's premier rock venue in 1972 but was closed again by 1975. It opened again two years later following a massive clean-up, under new management as a more efficient operation. The Stranglers were probably the first New Wave band to play there with Patti Smith in 1976 (on a later occasion they were banned for indecency by the GLC because of vocalist Hugh Cornwell exhibiting a tee shirt bearing the word Fuck). The Clash played a now-legendary gig where thousands of pounds worth of damage was done by fans tearing up hundreds of seats in order to crowd to the front of the stage. The theatre has now adopted the sensible policy of removing the front rows of seats to assist audience access.
In 1981 a smaller 'venue within a venue' was opened in the upstairs foyer of the Rainbow for smaller club-type events, this followed with a similar move being made in the downstairs foyer.

ROCK GARDEN (Club)
6-7 The Piazza, WC2
01-240 3961

Capacity: 200

The Rock Garden opened in July 1976 on the site of a late sixties Hippy cellar-type club called Middle Earth, in what has become the trendy centre of London's new Covent Garden redevelopment. Although its opening coincided with the advent of punk, it was conceived as a more general rock venue and initially 'nasty' new wave acts were shunned. It later relented, but revised its policy towards the more extreme bands when one of its doormen was stabbed in 1979. The Rock Garden now runs a progressive booking policy but its small size and awkward layout discourage the bigger names from playing there. Perhaps the Rock Garden's greatest night was when the Talking Heads chose to play their debut UK gig there in 1977.

THE ROXY (Now closed)
Neal Street, WC2

Capacity: 200

Formerly Chagaurama, a gay club, The Roxy opened its doors to punks on December 14 1976, Generation X played two sets. From January 1st 1977, managers Andrew Czezowski, Ralf Jedraszcyck and Barry Jones, were care takers to the astonishing explosion of music and lifestyle for which The Roxy was a catalyst and proving ground. Apart from The Sex Pistols, every important (and every unimportant) band of the period played The Roxy – as well as The Jam, The Damned, Siouxsie & The Banshees, Chelsea, Johnny Thunders & The Heartbreakers, Wire, The Slits, The Buzzcocks, The Adverts, etc., virtually anyone who phoned up and said that they had a band were given a chance to play. The club's suspended ceiling was gradually demolished by punks pogoing into it – the wall mirrors and furniture suffered similar fates. The club's toilets were soon established unisexually, and were frequently the setting for scenes often more outrageous than those onstage. It was THE punk place to a hang out, on nearly every night of the week you would find members of the new wave elite in the bar upstairs or in the audience downstairs. A pre-Pistols Sid Vicious would often be found, the worse for amphetamine and alcohol indulgence, perpertrating violence on anyone foolish enough not to see the joke.
After Czezowski lost control and interest in the place, it reopened under a less pioneering management and degenerated from degenerate-and-exciting to merely squalid and exploitative. It closed within 12 months.
The Roxy's early glory is partly captured on the EMI Harvest album 'The Roxy London WC2 (Jan – Apr 77)' (SHSP 4069) which features live tracks recorded by bands like Wire, The Buzzcocks, X-Ray Spex, The Adverts, etc., interspersed with comments and gossip from some of the club's patrons.

THE VENUE (Nightclub)
160 – 162 Victoria Street, SW1
01-834 5500

Capacity: 1280

Opened in November 1979, a former cinema and laserium, The Venue is a cavernous, American-style club owned by the Virgin Records company. Envisaged as a fairly upmarket operation, the realities of the British rock economy have turned what was a massive white elephant booking BOF-ish bands like Todd Rundgren, into a stronghold for futuristic, disco and newer wave attractions. The place still books in the occasional touring top-line British and US mainstream acts, but it has become a bit of a club of all trades, not yet a landmark for any particular type of music – but keeping pace with new wave, rockabilly and the rising tide of British jazz/funk.

THE VORTEX (Now closed)
Wardour Street, W1

Capacity: 400+

The Vortex was housed beneath Crackers, a disco pub, in what had been part of a failed 60s club and boutique complex. The layout featured a stage area and a number of bars linked by a small network of corridors; the resultant gothic atmosphere made the club extremely popular for punks of the second wind (it opened in the summer of 1977). The first wave of punk bands were being signed up at this time and hence the Vortex tended to feature the strugglers and the stragglers of the second rank – X-Ray Spex, Slaughter & The Dogs, Eater, Sham 69 and the still evolving Adam & The Ants and The Slits, ets.. The Vortex was run, very bodily, by John Miller, the ex-soldier who went on to achieve a small measure of notoriety by kidnapping trainrobber Ronnie Biggs in 1981. The Vortex lasted for just a year, and two rather lacklustre NEMS albums 'Live At The Vortex' Vols. 1 & 2, were released during its demise. That Sham 69 went on to be moderately successful is perhaps some acknowledgement to the Vortex's popularity.